PRAISE FOR *GET OFF THE X*

"As a former CIA intelligence officer, I can personally attest to the critical importance of getting off of X to accomplish our operational mission. Michele has masterfully parlayed this concept into this book, which will serve readers as an invaluable guide for navigating the uncertainties of life's journey with faith and resilience."

—Peter Warmka, founder of the Counterintelligence Institute and author of *Confessions of a CIA Spy*

"Profoundly important. . . . Michele reminds us that obstacles are not our problem. What ultimately defines our future success is how we respond to those challenges. Whether you are a singer, a CEO, or someone who has yet to find their way in the world, you can find purpose and meaning if you are willing to go where others won't. You must challenge yourself to live with uncertainty until the right door opens. Michele provides not only the inspiration to move through anxiety and fear but also the tools necessary to fight whatever is holding you back. It's time to stop waiting and wondering; get off the X and work for your dreams!"

—Howie Dorough, entrepreneur and member of Grammy-nominated group the Backstreet Boys

"*Get Off the X* is the perfect book to change the way you think about obstacles in your life. Michele's personal stories and advice for achieving your goals will make you motivated, happier, and more productive. I can't recommend this book enough."

—Eric DeCosta, executive vice president and general manager of the Baltimore Ravens

"The way Michele can make the complex simple breathes courage into thoughts and dreams that seem—quite frankly—impossible. *Get Off the X* helps you formulate a plan and then execute that plan step by step. That's how we bring the impossible into view. I found myself asking, 'Have I sold myself too short for too long?' There is no better time than now to get off the X. Let's GO!"

—Kendra Graham, RN, BSN, and wife of evangelist Will Graham

"*Get Off the X* is a page-turning book full of compelling stories and immensely practical steps to help you get unstuck! By sharing CIA strategies and military applications from her high-risk career, Michele provides clear direction to help you stride forward and away from that which is holding you back."

—Andy Searles, pastor of Church Together, professional sports chaplain, and community influencer

"I've had the privilege of hearing Michele Rigby Assad speak at our national symposium, and her insights are as sharp as they come. *Get Off the X* is not just another self-help book but a tactical guide from someone who's been in the trenches. If you're looking for a book that will push you to face your fears head-on and take decisive action, this is the one. Trust me, this is a book you'll want in your tool kit."

—Todd Kading, president and CEO of LeafHouse Financial

"In *Get Off the X*, Michele illuminates the idea that the biggest barriers to escaping the dangers of your comfort zone are not outside of you but in your own mind. I recommend this book to anyone looking for a breakthrough."

—Elizabeth Grace Saunders, time management coach and bestselling author of *How to Invest Your Time Like Money*, *Divine Time Management*, and *The 3 Secrets to Effective Time Investment*

"If you need a little motivation—and who doesn't?—well, here you go. It's like a pep talk from your smart, thoughtful friend . . . who just happens to have gained her wisdom as a CIA agent in remarkable circumstances. Michele Rigby Assad will get you moving."

—Brant Hansen, radio host and author of *Unoffendable*, *The Men We Need*, and *Life Is Hard, God Is Good, Let's Dance*

"The storytelling is so magnificent that you wind up reading a thriller without being aware that it is in fact an instruction manual for living your best life. Good luck trying to put it down before you've devoured the last page."

—Jack Barsky, former KGB agent and author of *Deep Undercover*

"In addition to giving us a window into her life, in this new adventure with *Get Off the X*, Michele helps us navigate our lives with less fear and more command. The thing about Michele is that she doesn't just dole out insights or subtle changes in perspective; she offers a complete paradigm shift when it comes to navigating those twists, turns, and devastating detours life can throw our way."

—Jade Simmons, CEO of Jade Media Global,
international speaker, and concert artist

"Everyone who reads *Get Off the X* will have a clear road map for confronting their fears, breaking free from stagnation, and achieving their goals. This book is a must-read for anyone seeking to navigate life's uncertainties—whether in personal growth, career advancement, or spiritual development—with resilience and purpose."

—Brittany Butler, former CIA targeting officer
and author of *The Syndicate Spy*

"I've now had the pleasure of reading both of Michele's books, and *Get Off the X* is the perfect complement to *Breaking Cover*. In the latter, Michele proves her bona fides as a true practitioner in the intelligence field. Her new book takes things to the next level, providing the reader with real-world lessons that can be applied anywhere, from the classroom to the boardroom to everyday life. An excellent addition to any bookshelf!"

—Dr. Vince Houghton, intelligence historian and author
of *The Nuclear Spies, Nuking the Moon,* and *Covert City*

"Enthusiasm is contagious. Faith is fire. And grit and determination are worth more than gold. *Get Off the X* is about having the courage to challenge the norm."

—Morgon Latimore, US Marine Corps veteran, change
enthusiast, professional endurance coach, and author of
Become an Amazing Coach and *Triathlete Mindset:
Aspire to Redefine What's Possible for You*

Also by Michele Rigby Assad:

Breaking Cover: My Secret Life in the CIA and What It Taught Me about What's Worth Fighting For

GET OFF THE

C.I.A. SECRETS FOR CONQUERING OBSTACLES AND ACHIEVING YOUR LIFE'S MISSION

MICHELE RIGBY ASSAD

604 Magnolia Lane
Nashville, TN 37211

Printed in United States of America.
First edition: 2024
10 9 8 7 6 5 4 3 2 1

ISBN: 978-1-947297-99-9 (Hardcover)
ISBN: 978-1-962435-00-0 (E-book)
ISBN: 978-1-962435-13-0 (Audiobook)

Publisher's Cataloging-in-Publication Data
Names: Assad, Michele Rigby, author.
Title: Get off the X : CIA secrets for conquering obstacles and achieving your life's mission / Michele Rigby Assad.
Description: Includes bibliographical references. | Nashville, TN: Dexterity, 2024.
Identifiers: ISBN: 978-1-947297-99-9 (hardcover) | 978-1-962435-00-0 (ebook) | 978-1-962435-13-0 (audiobook)
Subjects: LCSH Self-actualization (Psychology) | Success. | Goal (Psychology) | Conduct of life. | United States. Central Intelligence Agency. | Self-help. | BISAC SELF-HELP / Motivational & Inspirational | SELF-HELP / Personal Growth / Success | POLITICAL SCIENCE / Intelligence & Espionage
Classification: LCC BF637.S8. A77 2024 | DDC 158.1–dc23

To all of those trying to find their path

AUTHOR'S NOTE

A number of names and biographical details in this book have been altered to protect the identities of CIA sources, agency officers, and others who could be adversely affected by being associated with the CIA. Operational specifics such as locations, methodologies, and secret information have been redacted or obscured. Furthermore, the CIA's Prepublication Classification Review Board reviewed and provided clearance of this manuscript to ensure that no equities would be harmed through the publication of this material.

Details of CIA operations included in the book were initially captured in agency cables in which I documented meeting dynamics, intelligence acquisition, counterintelligence flags, and assessments. Since I am no longer employed by the agency, I do not retain access to these files and have had to recall those situations from memory.

The stories of family members and friends related in this book were based on personal interviews, in addition to documents they authored and shared with me that captured the details of those experiences.

All statements of fact, opinion, or analysis expressed in this book are my own and do not reflect the official position or views of the US government. Nothing in the contents should be construed as asserting or implying US government authentication of information or endorsement of my views.

CONTENTS

INTRODUCTION
HIGH-SPEED CHASE

"I think we're being followed."

Joseph was driving in a manner that alerted me to a potential problem, but now I knew why. He saw something that raised a red flag. It was an anomaly, something unusual and out of pattern.

Given the number of terrorists running around the city, we were on alert for hostile surveillance every time we got in the car. We didn't want to become an easy target for al-Qaeda operatives wanting to make a statement by executing Western officials. Neither did we want to be a target for tribesmen who sold kidnapped Westerners to terror groups for money or held them hostage to gain concessions from the government.

It was an exhausting way to live, always needing to be aware of our surroundings. But if we were going to come out of this tour alive, it had to be done.

Joseph kept peering in his rearview mirror while I looked in the side-view mirror, trying to catch a glimpse of the vehicle that had grabbed his attention.

In addition to being highly trained by the CIA to detect surveillance, Joseph had grown up in a police state. Because of that, he seemed to have a sixth sense for when he was being followed. As a Christian in Egypt, he had been harassed by kids wanting to beat him up and pursued by an Islamist school principal bent on assaulting him. Secret police loitered in and around churches to spy on sermons. Phone lines were monitored. You couldn't do much in Egypt without the authorities knowing where you were and what you were doing. Detecting surveillance was a survival skill that Joseph had unwittingly developed his whole life.

"It's a black Nissan Patrol, and he's been with us for several turns over the past few minutes."

In this country most drivers on the road were slow moving. So, to ferret out suspicious activity and determine whether we were being tailed by a hostile actor, Joseph drove faster and began to weave in and out of traffic. If the driver was not following us, then this simple strategy would create space between us.

Unfortunately, the vehicle in question followed suit. In the CIA we call this a *demeanor hit*, a behavioral indication that reveals a person's interest in you.

"Yeah, he's definitely with us," Joseph stated with a growing concern in his voice. For two CIA counterterrorism officers keenly aware of the terror threat around them, this development was wholly unwelcome. My heart raced as Joseph drove even faster. As the other vehicle responded in kind, Joseph said, "Hold on, I'm going to do my best to lose him."

We were not going to stick around and let this play out any longer. The singular focus was now to "get off the X" and away from danger. We were taught that we needed to do anything within our power to elude hostile entities targeting us. Since the car was the safest place to be, maneuvering away from the threat was the best course of action.

I swallowed hard as we bumped along at a high rate of speed on the city's poorly paved roads. Joseph said, "Okay, help me. The light is turning red, but we're going to try to blow through it. Any cars coming?"

I yelled, "Clear to the right. Go!"

The yellow light had already turned red, but we blew through the intersection.

What happened next further reinforced our fear that we were being chased: the other driver mirrored our actions and also flew through the intersection. We both exclaimed, "Oh no! He's still on us."

Every muscle in our bodies flexed. Every sense was focused on one thing and one thing alone: drive as though our lives depended on it. We both understood that we might be the target of an operation or attack, and we didn't want to stick around to find out.

To our dismay, another fifty meters in front of us was another light that had already turned red. Several cars in front of us were stopped at the light. To our left was a big curb and embankment, so Joseph maneuvered around the cars by driving up the curb onto the dirt embankment before steering back down onto the road and carefully winding our way through traffic at the red light.

The Nissan Patrol did the same.

As we approached yet another red light, our hearts raced with adrenaline and fear. Time seemed to slow as a significant amount of traffic ahead of us forced Joseph to slam on his brakes. Without warning, the pursuer, who was right on our bumper, crashed into the back of our SUV.

Our two vehicles seemed to bounce off each other slowly. The force of the collision caused the other vehicle to spin around our SUV, and it eventually landed in the middle of the intersection, facing us, about thirty feet away.

I was in shock, but Joseph was not. He quickly realized that our car was no longer operable. He shouted, "Look for guns! Look for guns!" fearing that the other occupant would emerge from his SUV with an AK-47. Before that driver could step out of the mangled wreck or we could scramble out of our broken vehicle, our cars were swarmed by hundreds of local men. The curious locals, quickly filling up the busy intersection, wanted to see who was in the cars and what was going on, a typical response to a car accident in that country. Whatever might have been planned was no longer possible with all the witnesses, chaos, and congestion that now separated and engulfed us.

PART 1: THE X

If we stay where we are, where we're stuck,
where we're comfortable and safe, we die there. . . .
When nothing new can get in, that's death.

—Anne Lamott, *Help, Thanks, Wow*

An ambush is defined by the US Army as "a surprise attack from a concealed position on a moving or temporarily halted target."[1] The ambush location is chosen for the advantage it conveys which includes the topography, elevation, existence of cover or concealment, and available escape routes. An ambush is used to "stop, deny, or destroy enemy forces by maximizing the element of surprise" and minimizing the ability of the enemy to respond to the provocation.

CHAPTER ONE
DEFINING THE X: HOW TO SURVIVE AN AMBUSH

If you want to survive, you must move.

—CIA instructors

I'll never forget the conversation Joseph, my husband and newly minted CIA operations officer, and I had when we were considering locations for our first posting. We spent many hours ranking the countries we were open to working in. When he threw out the name of ██████,* I winced. But as we continued to banter about the uniqueness of that locale, the idea of that posting grew on us. It appealed to the new intelligence officers because it was so far off the beaten path. It was a unique destination that held an allure for travelers who wanted to stretch themselves.

Although it was in a dangerous corner of the globe famous for carjackings and kidnappings, tribal skirmishes, and weapons bazaars, we were drawn in by its mystery. We also knew that counterterrorism work in this country was critical in the shadow of September 11, 2001. Despite all the uncertainty and fear, this was the ultimate opportunity to learn and grow. We were taking

*Country name redacted by the CIA.

a huge risk by choosing such a difficult first assignment, but we decided to go ahead and bid on it. Before long, we found out that we got the posting. Adventure we were seeking, and adventure it would be.

The CIA officers who preceded us were sent to places with very different cultures and political realities. These officers prepared to engage in operations that advanced our intelligence objectives while preserving the delicate political balance of the Cold War. Officers learned how to operate using calculated movements and careful counterintelligence strategies. Then, with the collapse and disintegration of the Soviet Union, everything changed. The Cold War came to an abrupt end, resulting in the contraction of the intelligence community and a significant decrease in its size and global presence.

As we all know, the critical need for good intelligence came roaring back to life on the heels of September 11. Only now we were facing a different kind of foe, not one we mingled with at cocktail parties or diplomatic soirees. CIA officers were being sent to nooks and crannies all over the world that had been ignored or overlooked for years. We were being sent to countries where Americans stood out like sore thumbs, where outsiders were not only mistrusted but were also assumed to be the enemy. Our assignments were no longer concerned with carefully building influence and power but learning how to execute counterterrorism operations in powder-keg environments.

Given these drastic operational changes, the CIA had the responsibility to prepare its staff for assignments in dangerous places. The agency provided weapons qualifications and counter-ambush training to every person assigned to temporary or permanent duty in a war zone and other high-risk locations. We had to prepare for the worst: we had to know how to survive a criminal ambush, kidnapping attempt, or terror attack. CIA paramilitary instructors called this personal security training "get off the X."

The X stands for the location targeted by enemies as they launch their attack; this is the place of our greatest vulnerability.

Our instructors taught us that, in the face of a surprise attack, people will respond in one of three ways: fight, flight, or freeze. Instructors emphasized that the training was preparing us to do anything but freeze. If you don't get off the X and you remain in the kill zone of a well-designed and well-executed ambush, you will probably die. But you can maximize your chance for survival if you move off the X and away from your attackers as quickly as possible.

In get-off-the-X training, instructors worked hard to mimic a real-life attack. They used flash-bang grenades and real weapons fitted with simunitions. They even dressed the part, covering their faces with black masks. The objective was to teach students how to maximize their chance for survival if ambushed. Students were told to do whatever was necessary to get off the X. The ultimate goal was to teach the students to push past their fear and develop the muscle memory to move and survive.

If you are in an operable vehicle, your best bet is to drive off the X. But if your engine is blown out by a grenade or your tires are deflated, you need to exit your vehicle and run for cover. The swifter your response, the better. This isn't easy, because in the first few moments of an attack, your mind races to make sense of what is happening. Confusion floods the mind and stress hormones flood the body. The longer it takes a person to act, the more dangerous the situation becomes. Fight or flight are positive responses. Shock is the enemy. Delay can mean death, and freezing on the X will get you killed.

During our first tour in ████████,* Joseph and I used our counter-ambush training to save ourselves when that other driver pursued us through clogged streets, red lights, and steep

*Country name redacted by the CIA.

embankments. We didn't know whether we were at risk of kidnapping or worse. But what we *did* know was that our training worked.

We were in a country where the foreigner was almost always declared responsible for traffic accidents and altercations, but the police declared the other driver at fault in our situation. They refused, however, to provide details uncovered in their investigation. They would not say what the driver was doing or what his objectives were. They would not disclose whether we had been strategic or opportunistic targets. Only after we pushed hard for answers did authorities admit that the local national, a man in his mid-twenties, had connections to senior government officials. Whatever he may have been planning would never be revealed to us.

The training had possibly saved our lives. And it would be used several times during that posting. I would soon realize that the critical skills of getting off the X matter not only in a war zone but wherever you live or work, as well. This security concept—conquering the tendency to freeze in the face of fear, difficulty, or shock—applies in ways you would never imagine.

CHERYL'S STORY: WELCOME TO THE JUNGLE

Cheryl and three of her CIA colleagues had decided to go hiking one weekend in the mountains that surround [redacted].* They planned to make the most of their time in this beautiful country, spending a few hours enjoying the great outdoors before returning to their hotel that Saturday afternoon. The group made this decision despite being warned of the extreme kidnapping risk where they were. They reasoned that a short hike on a well-worn path would not put them in harm's way. This was the capital, after all, a relatively safe place in comparison to cities where kidnapping was all the rage.

---

*City name redacted by the CIA.

After hiking for a couple of hours, the four sat down to rest and eat a snack. About twenty minutes into the rest stop, their pleasant conversation was interrupted by strange sounds. The popping of twigs and small branches caught their attention. They looked up to see three men emerge from the jungle. In a matter of seconds, the group was surrounded. The men were pointing guns at them and yelling in Spanish.

A litany of questions ran through their minds. Were they being robbed? What did the men want?

The frightened colleagues motioned toward their belongings to suggest that the men take whatever they desired. The men grabbed the bags and took the cash out of their wallets, but that wasn't what they came for. It quickly became clear that the well-armed men were not just robbing, but also kidnapping them. What had seemed like an innocent hike up the mountain had taken a terrible turn for the worse.

The kidnappers forced the two men and two women to collect their belongings and march farther up the mountain. They slowly made their way, minds swirling, they wondered they were going and what they could do to stop an already bad situation from spiraling further out of control. Because of their training, they knew they had to get off the X, but the men's guns were trained on their backs. The muzzles of the guns were thrust into them every now and then to enforce compliance and encourage them to pick up the pace.

After a couple of grueling hours, the group arrived at a small clearing. The men motioned for them to take off their pants and remove their shoes. Bracing for the worst, the group complied, each one praying for deliverance from what was to come next. They soon realized that the reason for the forced disrobement was not because they were going to be assaulted but because the kidnappers knew it would be hard for them to escape in their undergarments and without any shoes. After the clothing was confiscated, the group sat barefoot in their undergarments, waiting.

Over the next hour or so, Cheryl and one of her male colleagues did their best to assess the situation and share their thoughts in barely audible whispers. They had enough Spanish to work out that the people who'd kidnapped them were not members of the [redacted],* who often held their victims for months or even years.

Instead, the kidnappers were trying to negotiate their sale to the feared insurgent group. Trying desperately to listen in on their captors' phone calls and heated discussions, the CIA officers figured out that the kidnappers were biding their time at this location, awaiting an exchange of money for their valuable American hostages.

Between phone calls, the man who seemed to be the leader walked over to Cheryl's colleague Sarah, who was lying on the ground with her hands tied behind her back. He took out his revolver, spun the cylinder, and placed the muzzle against her head. As the group held their breath in horror, he pressed the trigger. Instead of the explosion of a round, there was an empty click. There wasn't a round in the chamber.

He laughed diabolically and then walked away from the terrified captives. In that moment, Sarah's countenance completely changed. Her eyes went blank. Even though the weapon hadn't fired, the stress of thinking she was about to die drained the life right out of her. "She completely checked out," Cheryl later recalled. "What was left was just the shell of a person."

The man continued to taunt the group by repeating this terrifying exercise. Each time he put the weapon to someone's head, cocked the hammer, and pulled the trigger, nothing happened except for the almost imperceptible click. It seems that he'd never put a round in the chamber. The members of the group assumed they were worth more alive than dead.

---

*Insurgent organization name redacted by the CIA.

Finally tiring of the torturous game, the man walked away from the clearing to take more phone calls out of earshot. One of the other kidnappers accompanied him. The remaining captor was told to watch the group, which he did half-heartedly.

Minutes passed, and since the group could no longer see two of the captors, they realized that this was the opening they'd hoped for. Cheryl and the two men loosened and then removed each other's bindings without being noticed by the sentry. As they whispered the plans to one another, one thing was clear: Sarah had already given up. She was incapable of communicating with them or doing anything to help herself or anyone else. They'd have to drag her away.

With the guard's back turned and the others still out of sight, one of them whispered, "Let's go!"

They grabbed Sarah's arms and pulled her up off the ground and scurried into the jungle as fast as their bare feet could carry them. As soon as the guard realized what was happening, he began shouting in Spanish for his compatriots. The escapees could hear his shouts and the cacophony of screaming voices in the distance.

The group didn't know how much of a lead they had, only that they needed to get down that mountain posthaste. The captors were in hot pursuit, streaming down the mountain and shooting haphazardly into the thick forest. Even though the men couldn't see their targets, they could still discharge rounds of ammunition in their direction. Cheryl's and her colleagues' ears were filled with the expletives of their pursuers and the spine-chilling sound of errant rounds whizzing by, hitting trees and exploding bark into the thick, humid air.

The group didn't have the luxury of looking back or assessing their progress. Cheryl and her colleagues surged forward despite the uncertainty of their ability to outrun the kidnappers. Compounding their stress was the increasingly dark and foreboding jungle they had to negotiate.

Their progress was sometimes swift as they ran as fast as their legs could carry them, and at other times, excruciatingly slow. In places, the jungle was so thick they could barely wend themselves through it. They picked their way through thickets and thorn-bushes, proceeding inches at a time. They maneuvered in and around tangled roots. They crawled over logs in their underwear and navigated the uneven forest floor without shoes. But they maintained their singular focus to escape. Cheryl later recalled that the only thing running through her mind was *just keep going.*

Hours after breaking away from their captors, the group pushed through the jungle wall and suddenly emerged onto a city street. Despite extreme fear and physical exhaustion, they made it. They had done the impossible: they had extracted themselves from a kidnapping and months or years of captivity.

Against all odds, the CIA officers had managed to get off the X. Cheryl and her two male colleagues had kept their wits and acted in a timely manner. Although scratched up and covered in dirt, sweat, and blood, they had made their way down the mountain, over and under myriad obstacles to freedom . . . glorious freedom.

Getting off the X is a critical skill when you work as a special operative in a dangerous country. But this concept is just as important no matter where you live or what you do. It's applicable outside the CIA and is the key to moving yourself forward no matter what circumstance conspires to hold you back.

CHAPTER TWO
GETTING OFF THE X: THE METAPHOR

The credit belongs to the man who is actually in the arena, whose face is marred by dust and sweat and blood; who strives valiantly . . . and who at the worst, if he fails, at least fails while daring greatly, so that his place shall never be with those cold and timid souls who know neither victory nor defeat.

—Theodore Roosevelt, "Citizenship in a Republic"

Life is a tug-of-war between the lightning speed of change in our postmodern world and our own physiology—bodies wired to conserve energy to survive. Anything that challenges this efficient, well-worn circuitry requires the output of energy and effort. And let's face it: life is a daily confrontation with glitches, troubles, questions, and dilemmas, whether planned or unexpected and unwelcome. Instead of facing security-related obstacles such as tribesmen or insurgent groups, we face options and obstacles that force us to ponder our next steps. How you view such decision points is critical.

Consider the possibility that the most difficult obstacles aren't the circumstances themselves but how we respond to them. The biggest giants we face are the glass ceilings we erect and the false narratives we construct about what we can and cannot do. It's the stories we tell ourselves about what is possible. When we allow the forces of fear, uncertainty, or intimidation to get the best of us or simply don't know how to react, we end up sitting squarely on the seat of the status quo or languishing in the center of our comfort zones.

The longer we sit on that X and entertain those false narratives, the harder it becomes to move. This concept is explained in physics as Newton's first law of motion: an object at rest remains at rest and an object in motion remains in motion at constant speed and in a straight line unless it is acted on by an external force. The tendency to resist change is inertia.

Inertia is strong. It keeps us glued to the ground like a mouse on a sticky trap. Humans have a proclivity to remain in that steady, stable, dependable spot because it takes a great deal of energy to overcome inertia and *move.*

I don't know about you, but I love the comfort zone. It's warm and toasty there! I am a creature of habit, and I love a good, predictable schedule. Contrary to what my career trajectory and travel history would suggest, I'm a homebody who values routine. I like to know what to expect. Change is difficult for me. I have to consciously push myself to try new things and force myself to brave the unknown.

But because I've been willing to challenge these natural predilections, I've become proficient at getting off the X. I don't permit negative feelings to persist and hold me hostage; I've learned not to bend to their will. Despite extreme intimidation, I applied to the CIA and braved the clandestine training program to serve as an operative. Despite a fear of living and working in war zones, I accepted postings to Baghdad and three other locations at the front lines of the war on terror. Despite uncertainty, after ten years in the CIA I made the bold decision to leave the agency and kick off an international consulting and speaking career. None of these decisions were easy. In fact, I would describe them as excruciating. But what I have been able to achieve in the wake of those decisions has been beyond my wildest dreams.

Because it was so hard for me to figure out how to get off the X, I am passionate about helping others find their way, too. The challenges I have repeatedly faced in trying to move forward are not unique. Life is full of unknowns, setbacks, and obstacles, and we are continually faced with the challenge of how to push past them. Getting off the X is less about figuring out what to do and more about having the courage and resilience to employ various options until you find an operational approach that works. It's about getting back up when you fall, when you don't hit your objective. It's about not capitulating to opposition, but understanding that you must keep pressing forward toward your goals, come hell or high water. It's resetting your brain to realize that setbacks are mere bumps on the road to your next big thing.

This book tells stories of many who faced great difficulties in achieving their life's mission, and demonstrates how they overcame circumstances that conspired to diminish their drive. That's what this book is about: diagnosing what's keeping you on the X so that you can plot and execute your way off it. The following chapters reveal CIA methodologies that will empower you to plan operations, manage risk, steady your focus, and execute well. These are simple yet effective intelligence tricks you can apply to everyday life, both personally and professionally, to break the impasses and get off the X.

CHAPTER THREE

AM I ON THE X?

I believe every human has a finite number of heartbeats.
I don't intend to waste any of mine.

—Neil Armstrong

A couple of weeks after Joseph and I arrived in Baghdad for our third CIA tour, the Counter-Rocket, Artillery, Mortar (C-RAM) system was activated by incoming rockets. C-RAM systems were first deployed in Iraq and Afghanistan to provide a warning to ground forces and forward operating bases that incoming rockets, artillery, or mortar rounds had been detected. At our compound in Baghdad, the system was set up to sound the alarm once projectiles were detected midair. This forewarning gave us time to get into a bunker or a hardened facility before they hit the ground and exploded.

Joseph and I were new to the war game, so this little exercise of running to the bunkers was weird and unfamiliar. The C-RAM was connected to loudspeakers positioned all around the compound that sounded the alarm, "Wonk! Wonk! Wonk!" The siren was followed by a voice that warned, "Incoming. Incoming. Incoming."

The C-RAM gave us several seconds to get to a bunker if we weren't already in a building that could withstand those types of air strikes. The bunkers were spread out all over the compound, so there was a solid chance of reaching one before the projectiles hit and exploded. Once inside, you'd brace yourself for the inevitable boom and attendant shock waves that rippled out from the point of impact. If you were close enough, the shock wave would knock you to the ground. Otherwise, it simply shook the earth beneath you.

It's funny how certain things stick in your mind forever, while something that happened yesterday slips away so easily. That first C-RAM experience in Baghdad has been one of those lasting memories for me. It felt otherworldly running to the already-full bunker outside the cafeteria. We were shoved in there like sardines, uncomfortably close to people we didn't know, shoulder to shoulder and nose to nose with twenty officers and local Iraqi staff. It was July, so to say it was hot and uncomfortable is a massive understatement.

The rocket that night hit a munitions depot a couple of miles away, so instead of one big explosion, the rocket initiated a domino effect of a large detonation followed by a series of smaller explosions as the munitions "cooked off." It was like fireworks on the Fourth of July. I had to remind myself that this wasn't a controlled detonation but an uncontrolled event, dangerous to those in close proximity. The unstable cook-off required us to remain in the bunker for a long time until security staff could ascertain that we were no longer in any danger.

My mind raced as we stood in the cramped bunker waiting for the "all clear" announcement. What was this new life we had been unceremoniously thrown into? I'd never been in a bunker before. I'd never even considered going into the military, yet here I was serving in a war zone and being exposed to all kinds of things I'd never thought about. That night I was baptized into the life of a war-zone officer.

Because that first strike missed our compound and landed a comfortable distance away from us, I remember thinking, *Well, that wasn't too bad.*

I exhaled, letting the stress leave my body with the premature assumption that this was what rockets did; they stayed far enough away not to be a real concern.

Over the next month or so, I learned how ignorant that was. The Green Zone was the target of an increasing number of rockets and mortars. Previously, Iraqi Shia insurgents had aimed the rockets in our direction but rarely hit anything. Once Iranian experts taught them how to home in on their targets, what had been out of reach was now squarely in the crosshairs.

Over time, we were enveloped by the strange theater of war: Sirens, bunker runs, and ground-shaking explosions increased as the rocket men turned up the heat. Pretty soon we became experts at getting to safety quickly, no matter where we were located on the compound.

Several months after Joseph and I arrived in Baghdad for our yearlong tour, terrorism, militant operations, and sectarian cleansing hit a fever pitch, with volleys of up to nine rockets at a time. We were running to the bunkers numerous times a day. Sprinkle in a car bomb or two, and the atmosphere was thick with the blaring of sirens, shaking, and rumbling. On top of everything else, the emotional toll of knowing dozens of people were injured or killed with each explosion was difficult to bear.

Sleep is always difficult in a war zone. The sounds of far-off explosions often punctured the night, and then before anyone could get a sufficient amount of shut-eye, the first siren of the day sounded around 6:00 a.m.—the worst alarm clock in the world: "Wonk! Wonk! Wonk! Incoming. Incoming. Incoming."

Those of us on permanent duty watched a steady stream of newcomers arrive and depart days, weeks, or months later. If they didn't know where the bunkers were, they learned fast. They also learned that you went to bed wearing something you didn't mind your colleagues seeing later in the bunker.

Those poor people. They had bags under their eyes and walked around like zombies. Between the jet lag, bunker runs, daily car bombs, and random explosions, they weren't sleeping much. I remember one officer crawling under her desk one day, desperate for a catnap. She was too scared to go back to the trailer-like sleeping pods since it was "rocket time," the period each afternoon when the insurgents volleyed a battery of rockets at us in the Green Zone.

One of the new recruits, who was quickly becoming a good friend, begged to understand. "How do you do this? How are you not coming apart at the seams?"

I realized then that it wasn't the newcomers who were strange as they struggled to adapt. It was us: we were the weirdos. We were living in an alternate reality that hadn't changed overnight but deteriorated over time. We had slowly adapted to the unusual circumstances and hadn't realized how bizarre the situation had become. The war-zone conditions we faced every day reminded me of the story about a frog in boiling water: If you drop a frog into a pot of boiling water, it will immediately jump out to save itself. But if you put the frog into a pot of tepid water and slowly turn up the heat, the frog will slowly adapt to the rising temperature and will not have the awareness or wherewithal to escape. The frog will die because it doesn't perceive the danger and doesn't save itself from the impending rolling boil.

We were the frogs dropped into a pot of water whose temperature had been increased so imperceptibly that we didn't realize we were now swimming in a cauldron. New to this madness, our recently arrived colleagues did not find the rolling boil a welcome place to be and were ready to jump out.

How often do we sit on the X, oblivious to the climbing temperature? How often do we normalize our station in life when it's no longer serving our interests? How often do we acculturate to situations that do not benefit us and, in fact, threaten our long-term well-being? How often do we give up our dreams because we're flying on autopilot? Realizing how easy it is to lounge on the comfort of my routine, I regularly ask myself, *Am I sitting on the X right now? Am I a frog in boiling water?*

WHAT THE X FEELS LIKE

There are two kinds of people in the world: those who know they're stuck on the X and are working to get off it, and those who have no idea they've stagnated.

If you are in the former group, you are desperate to figure out what's next in your life. Maybe you don't know your ultimate purpose. You have searched here and there and still don't know what you are supposed to be doing. Maybe you're like I was in my twenties, constantly mining for clues to your future. Maybe you've applied to every job opportunity under the sun and still have nothing to show for your extensive efforts. This kind of X is the most frustrating because you are trying your darndest but are still looking uncertainty in its big ugly face. Waves of disappointment and doubt flood your mind as you try to summon the energy and focus to keep trudging forward.

Or maybe circumstances have thrown you on the X and you are stunned, wondering how to respond. You are having to recalibrate, relearn how to dream, and even reconceptualize your place in the world. Maybe you are farther along. After events forced you onto the X, you've come out of a period of shock or grief; you know you're ready to move forward, but you don't know where to start. In these situations, fear and anxiety rule the day.

If you are in the latter group, unaware you're stuck, here are some indicators that it's time to consider your next move:

- Are your energy levels off? Do you feel less interested or motivated than you used to be? Bored with the status quo? Worried that you're not growing or developing anymore?
- Is it hard to get out of bed? Do you wake up dreading the day but are unable to pinpoint why?
- Do you feel an uneasiness staying the current course but haven't wanted to admit it to yourself?

Don't push back these feelings of doubt or unease. Your gut is trying to tell you something. These indicators are conspiring to show you that it's time for a change.

The next question is this: What will your response be?

RESPONSES TO THE X

Everyone finds themselves on the X at some point. It's not wrong or unnatural. The X is a normal part of life. It's the natural in-between, the pregnant pause where we're not quite sure how to move a difficult initiative forward. The X is the closure of an era and the questioning of what comes next. It's the moment we realize we are no longer being served by what was once exciting or good for us.

When we approach the X in a healthy manner, it is a thought provoker. It's a waypoint to a new destination. The problem is not finding ourselves on the X but getting stuck there. We want the X to inspire questions and propel us forward. When we don't heed the call, the X turns into a dead end. That is what we want to avoid.

It's helpful to assess where you are now so that you can plot your subsequent moves. Which of the following categories best describes your current state of affairs?

- *Danger Zoners*: This is the category of people who are content with the X. They may have tried to get unstuck but gave up too early, letting their fears get the best of them. Perhaps they lacked the stamina to try new strategies or the perseverance to survive the dreaded in-betweens. They have resigned themselves to this danger zone, which becomes a dead zone over time.
- *Developmentals*: In spy speak, a "developmental" is a person you are trying to recruit as a spy. Developmentals recognize they're stuck but don't know what to do about it. They need a little push, a little encouragement to realize that getting off the X is a mission we are all capable of.
- *Trainees*: Trainees are formally recruited—primed for change and thirsty for adventure. They are signed up to decode the secrets of tradecraft and work diligently to find their next step. They are ready to discover their next project or their life's mission.
- *Experienced operatives*: I'm off that X and running, sister! This category is for all who have learned how to get unstuck and are ready to serve as agents of influence and help others do the same.

The key to moving forward is to understand where you are, why you're stuck, and what's holding you hostage on the X. Only then can you do something about it.

PART 2: DENIAL AND DECEPTION

A nation can survive its fools, and even the ambitious.
But it cannot survive treason from within.

—attributed to Marcus Tullius Cicero

In the cloak-and-dagger world of espionage, a denial and deception (D&D) operation seeks to deny the enemy accurate information about your capabilities, activities, or true intentions and replace it with false data or disinformation. D&D operations are designed to shape an adversary's assessments and trigger them to act in particular ways, to give the instigator the security, military, or economic advantage.

An effective D&D campaign denies the truth and replaces it with a false narrative. It degrades the vision needed to move in the right direction. It prevents you from seeing clearly, narrowing your focus and sending you to the wrong place. The allure of a good deception carefully draws you in and holds you tightly in its grip. It plays on your fears and biases while exploiting your hopes and dreams. D&D campaigns erode your capacity to execute effective operations.

CHAPTER FOUR
INTIMIDATION

If you give in to intimidation, you'll go on being intimidated.

—Aung San Suu Kyi, winner of the 1991 Nobel Peace Prize

The dictionary defines *intimidate* as "to make timid or fearful . . . to compel or deter by threats."[2] Intimidation is an insidious mental obstacle that thwarts your ability to get off the X by shifting your focus onto your alleged insufficiency. Intimidation waves the warning flag: "Danger! Danger! Don't go there. You're not good enough. You're not smart enough. You don't know how to do that. You might fail."

Intimidation is an internal D&D campaign that makes you settle for less than you are capable of. You end up playing it safe because intimidation lies to you about your talent and potential. It causes you to deride developmental opportunities that might reveal unknown giftings. Intimidation encourages you to place too much emphasis on what other people think or how you rank against some perceived measure of fitness for the task.

Intimidation is an ambition killer that seeks solace in mediocrity. The voice that whispers the musings of intimidation in your head cannot be trusted. I know this because intimidation has betrayed me at every turn. Looking back, I can see that all of its warnings were much ado about nothing. Those lies could have cost me an extraordinary life and career. I am glad I didn't heed them.

THE UGLY LITTLE TROLL

Intimidation acts as an ugly little troll that stubbornly plants itself on my shoulder, whispers in my ear, and hounds me with each life development. I have perpetually struggled with intimidation when faced with new activities or life chapters. Ever since I was a little girl, I have given too much leeway to the voice of pragmatism and hesitation.

In elementary school I remember watching my closest friends and classmates board the bus one day each week for their transport from Triangle Elementary to a gifted program in Howey-in-the-Hills, Florida. They learned all kinds of fun things in the gifted program while I remained with the other students in the regular classroom.

I wasn't on the bus, so I knew I wasn't as smart as they were. I found out as an adult that I'd been tested but didn't pass the exam. My sister, Julie, did pass and got to board the gifted bus, which further added to my sense that I was smart but not *that smart.* I got straight As, but I wasn't truly *gifted.*

The perception of being "less than" didn't always tell me the truth, yet I carried it with me with such commitment. In high school I was sure that I knew my place in the pecking order. It's not hard to look around at the test scores and accomplishments of your classmates and see how much better they are at math and English. Despite all my hard work, there was no way on God's green earth I was going to pass the calculus Advanced Placement™ test for college. (True. My results were abysmal.)

Despite my diligent work, my essays simply weren't going to be chosen for publication in the literary catalog. (True.)

Yet something about my self-perception was off. At graduation I tied with Heather M. to be salutatorian of my class. That should have taught me to stop selling myself short. But I picked that ugly troll right back up and carried it on my shoulder throughout university. My scores on my second SAT were just high enough for me to be awarded an honors scholarship to attend Palm Beach Atlantic University in West Palm Beach, Florida. Knowing that I barely slid into the honors program, I understood that everyone else in honors class was smarter than I was. Society told us that standardized test scores and grades were the ultimate judges of our potential.

After graduating from university, getting married, and moving to Washington, DC, the place of big brains and even bigger egos, can you guess what I did? I kept that little intimidation monster close—right there on my shoulder where it had always been. If you want to feel small, try to look for a job on Capitol Hill with all the other type A overachievers.

This self-limiting malady may be due in part to my high levels of emotional intelligence—I am extremely cognizant of what I don't know or don't understand. Therefore, I don't live in a place of false, ego-driven assumptions about myself. No, sir! No entitlement issues here. My situation is quite the opposite. I am keenly aware of my limitations.

For that reason, I don't grasp my talents and capabilities until they are fully developed and strikingly obvious. I assume everyone else has things figured out because they seem to function quite well and appear undeterred in their pursuit of the next big thing. When watching others jump headfirst into difficult situations, hard-to-get jobs, or complex projects, I assume they must be more capable, better equipped, and more intelligent because they look so confident.

COGNITIVE BIASES THAT HOLD US BACK

I have a hard time understanding new concepts until I've learned them forward and backward, inside and out. Until the moment that the knowledge I carefully process clicks, I'm barely mediocre, and fully intimidated by the task. But when I get it, I *really* get it. Socrates said that the only true wisdom is knowing when you know nothing. That would make me a very wise woman.

If you are surrounded by people who appear to be confident in their knowledge, experience, or ideas, and you yourself do not feel that way, your self-perception could be deeply flawed because you're subconsciously comparing yourself with those individuals. People with high levels of emotional intelligence tend to interpret others' confidence as evidence of their expertise; therefore, it might be helpful to understand a cognitive bias called the *Dunning-Kruger effect*. This refers to a lack of self-awareness that causes people with limited knowledge to overestimate their competence.[3] The phrase that reflects this bias is, "I think I know; therefore I'm an expert!" Conversely, high performers tend to underestimate their abilities. They often limit or hold themselves back, aware of the depth and breadth of knowledge required to be well versed on a topic. Cracking the code of the Dunning-Kruger effect could prevent you from degrading the self-assessment of your potential and sticking to the X.

Researchers have observed this cognitive bias when participants were asked about their performance on a test. Before the test takers were told their scores, they were asked to assess how they did: Those in the lowest 25 percent ranked themselves as having performed near the top. Conversely, people who performed in the top 25 percent ranked themselves as having performed lower than they did.[4] This mindset could explain why so many of us don't lean in and pursue opportunities, because they seem unrealistic or out of reach. Our self-perception is skewed.

Studies have also shown that women tend to downplay their performance and contributions, and men tend to have a positivity bias, which causes them to overestimate their past performances. This difference in perception can cause women to be less confident and men more confident.[5]

I have allowed my own cognitive bias to color my perception of the world and my place in it. I have shrunk from opportunities, repeatedly assuming that everyone else knows more than I do. I was halfway through my CIA career before I realized that I was more knowledgeable about the Middle East than most of the people I had interacted with in the CIA, the US military, Congress, and the National Security Council.

Why didn't I grasp the level of my own expertise earlier? I had an advanced degree in Arab studies and had spent a semester studying in Cairo. I had traveled to Egypt, Israel, the West Bank, Morocco, and Kuwait. I had graduated from Georgetown University with a working knowledge of Arabic. For goodness' sake, I had even married into a Middle Eastern family. But I was keenly aware of all the things I *didn't* know. I was smart enough to understand the limits of my knowledge and experience but assumed that other people's confidence meant they knew more. That simply wasn't true.

A trivial but potent example of being intimidated by the confidence facade occurred for me at the tail end of the CIA's paramilitary training, right after we graduated from tradecraft training. It was the last day of the week and the last day of the module on high-performance driving. Students were pretty spent by that point, driving hard and fast all week. The last exercise involved maneuvering a car through a curvy course, the path set out for the drivers with little orange cones.

Once we made it to the end, we had to throw the car into reverse and complete the entire windy path backward, all the way to the starting line. Instructors timed us to see how quickly we could complete the challenge. For each cone we knocked down, a fraction of time was added to our overall finish. The point of the exercise was to challenge our ability to drive quickly but maintain full control of the vehicle by staying within the lines. A driver could technically finish first, but if they knocked down a few cones, they might place second or third. They couldn't just drive *fast*; they had to drive *well*. Throughout the week, instructors reminded students at every opportunity that high-performance driving is all about control. And they repeated the mantra "Smooth is fast."

I don't like doing things unless I can do them well. I am also highly competitive and like to win. I was so exhausted at the end of that week of training. The course looked confusing, and I wasn't even sure which cones we were supposed to follow. If I could have opted out of the scenario, I would have. (If I can't be good, I'm not going to do it.)

Several of my colleagues were whooping and hollering because they were going to show everyone else how to get it done. Those not making a big deal out of it were calm former law enforcement officers who presumably had gone through this kind of training at the academy. There was no way I was going to do this as well as the former special ops and law enforcement officers. Their displays of confidence had me second-guessing my driving skills and my ability to perform at the top of the class. I lowered my expectations and merely hoped that I wouldn't embarrass myself.

I was feeling so unengaged that I volunteered to go last. When it was my turn, I made my way to the car, exhaled out the nervous energy, climbed in, turned on the engine, and placed my hands on the wheel. I stared at the track in front of me and prepared for the go signal. One thing I excel at is focus. Even though I was tired and not feeling it, I forced myself to block out everything else and waited for the instructor as he counted down: "Three, two, one—go!"

I zipped off as fast as I could, trying hard to navigate around the curves and hairpin switchbacks while staying between the cones. Once I got to the end, I whipped that car into reverse and backed up all the way to the starting line, relieved I hadn't made a fool of myself. As I exited the car, I told the instructor, "I wasn't horrible."

The instructor replied, "No, you weren't horrible. You won."

"What? I won?" I asked, bemused. I thought maybe I hadn't heard right, or he was kidding.

"Yes! You knocked down only one cone, the very last one. A couple of the students who had quicker times knocked down three or four cones, so you have the best time. You are number one."

Moments like these remind me not to give up before I try. I have wasted too many opportunities because I didn't think I could win, rank the highest, or be among the best. I have opted out because I wasn't sure I had the talent or skills to deliver. Getting off the X requires a strategic effort to combat my natural inclination to bow out of opportunities because I'm hyperaware of my limitations and the restraints I place on myself.

If you are guilty of the same thing, it's time to change your mind, alter your thinking, and correct your perceptions so you don't miss out on the win. This mind shift has enabled me to unlink my assumptions about other people's capabilities based on their displays of confidence. You must dig a little deeper to explore what you are really bringing to the table. And most of the time you cannot know what you enjoy or what you're good at until you try.

WHEN COMPARISON HURTS: INSIDIOUS IMPOSTOR SYNDROME

One of the major contributors to the internal debate of "Can I do this?" is the issue of comparison. We look at the people who have already accomplished the task to determine whether we have what it takes. But what if you are nothing like the people in charge—those who are successful by virtue of their positions, promotions, or power?

When we make these comparisons and they don't hold up, we are stricken with impostor syndrome, the belief that we don't have the proper qualifications, skills, experience, or personality traits to excel in a place or position. Impostor syndrome makes us wonder how we got hired and when we'll get fired. It makes us question when the people in charge will realize they've made a big mistake and give us the boot. It makes us worry that we are not a *real* [fill in the blank] but someone parading as such. Impostor syndrome tells us that we'll never fit in and won't be able to fulfill our job responsibilities.

Such was the case when I started working at the CIA. I'd never felt like such a fish out of water. First, there was the general impression that the CIA was run by older white men who were too busy to talk to anyone, too important to mentor anyone, and too larger than life to answer to anyone. Many had permanent scowls on their faces and seemed to dislike interacting with other human beings. They were unapproachable and disagreeable.

During training, our class was sent to the CIA headquarters building in McLean, Virginia, for a couple of months on an interim assignment. This quick stint at headquarters gave us a chance to see how the concepts we were learning applied in real life. I was assigned to work with a branch of collection management officers (CMOs) in the Counterterrorism Center (CTC). The office was absolutely humming with activity in the wake of September 11, with everyone engaged in hunting down terrorists to prevent the next attack. The CTC was the busiest and most exciting place to be in the CIA.

Each trainee was assigned a headquarters mentor to help us learn the ropes of our temporary office jobs, and my mentor was a person named Susan. I knocked on the door of her office, anxious to make a good impression. Peering inside, I saw a middle-aged woman sitting at her desk. She had the appearance of the old *Saturday Night Live* character Pat, but with a big balding spot on her head. She motioned for me to come in and take a seat next to her desk. She pulled the chair uncomfortably close to hers.

After I sat down and took stock of Susan's office, I realized that something was off.

Everywhere I looked I saw *Buffy the Vampire Slayer*. There were Buffy action figures, Buffy posters, Buffy coffee cups, Buffy mouse pads, Buffy calendars, and Buffy photographs. Susan's office was draped in Buffy swag in every conceivable form. All I could get out of my mouth at that point was the insightful "So I guess you like Buffy?"

Susan laughed.

I was slightly uncomfortable, but at least she was friendly. Susan warmly welcomed me to the branch and started explaining something about the job. Her introductory speech was interrupted numerous times by officers sticking their heads into the office and asking questions. Each time they came to the door, I tried to inch my chair away. And each time she would turn back to me and pull my chair closer to see something on the computer screen. I couldn't shake the weirdness of this whole scene.

I can't remember much of that introductory conversation with Susan, but I distinctly remember that my head was spinning. I kept thinking, *This is what a senior CMO is like?* Susan's expressed fascination and strange obsession with Buffy was weird, to say the least. And her knowledge of the most esoteric facts related to the handling, distribution, and clearance of secret intelligence reports froze my blood. I thought, *Oh my God. Is this what I need to know? Is this what I'm supposed to aspire to?*

I didn't find Susan's job the least bit interesting. And, of course, I just couldn't shake the feeling that Susan herself was odd—one of the strangest human beings I'd ever met. Those few months at headquarters gave me real pause. I didn't fit in with the leadership I saw in the building, and now I seemed to have nothing in common with a well-respected senior CMO either. Maybe I wasn't the only trainee who struggled with this, but in the moment, it sure felt like it, because no one else expressed any misgivings. Most of the other recruits seemed to be taking to their new jobs quickly and easily. I had to wonder, *What's wrong with me? Why can't I just feel comfortable like everyone else?*

The experience at headquarters was not an encouraging one. I couldn't understand how I could grow in a place where I didn't enjoy aspects of the work others seemed interested in. Thankfully, I didn't let it deter me. These comparisons were logical, but I harbored an irrepressible optimism that maybe there was more to the story. Maybe things would get better.

What I later learned in the school of hard knocks was that there *was* a completely different way to approach my job. Many CMOs, like Susan, took the administrative approach, which focused on the coding and distribution of reports. I took the operational one, which focused on the acquisition and sourcing of reports. I focused less on *how* information was packaged and more on the *quality* of the information coming in. I wasn't thinking about cable systems or debates on report classification. I preferred to delve into our sources and their identities and access, to ensure we were working with the right people to get the best intelligence.

Evaluating intelligence from this angle fascinated and invigorated me. This focus opened up a whole new world of exploring the existence of intelligence fibbers, fabricators, and double agents. My work as a CMO in the field enabled me to find ways to make that position fit my preferences and personality. I found a way to make it mine, to bring my personal strengths to the fore and apply them in a way that was not just fun but desperately needed. The world was changing, and the amount of intelligence streaming in was off the charts. In the wake of September 11, people came out of the woodwork with "information on al-Qaeda." The quicker you could ferret out the good sources from the bad sources, the better.

Both approaches were required for the mission, but that wasn't initially clear to me in training or in my interim assignment. I had to stick around long enough to develop my own unique approach to CMO operations. By not giving up too early, I was able to push the boundaries of the job, expand what I was permitted to do, and engage in a meaningful way that remade the box I kept getting stuck in.

The lesson here is to not let comparisons intimidate you or hold you back. Stop assuming that you are defined by that which came before. You are not here to fit into a mold; you're here to switch things up. As my friend Jenny Blake always says, "If change is the only constant, then let's get better at it." Those who seek to change the world aren't afraid of searching for a better approach. They set a new tone. They discover better methods. They bring their authentic selves to the problem and crush the challenges of a constantly changing environment. New problems require new ways of thinking to come up with new solutions.

WHEN COMPARISON HELPS: THE POWER OF POSITIVE ROLE MODELS

When Joseph was bidding for our first tandem overseas assignment, I had a serious discussion about the upcoming tour with Stacy, a CIA colleague and one of my best friends. She was working as an al-Qaeda targeter and had been among the first officers to serve in Afghanistan immediately after September 11. Stacy and I were very much alike: overachievers from small towns who had studied the Arab world.

We were taking a walk together on a Northern Virginia hiking trail when I asked Stacy one of the most important questions I'd ever posed: "Stacy, given your experience serving abroad, do you think I can I do this? Do I have what it takes?"

Without missing a beat, she replied, "Yes, absolutely."

"Really? Because you know me, Stacy. I trust you."

"Yes, Michele. I wouldn't say that unless I meant it. You can totally do this job."

She went on to warn me about the parts of the job I probably wouldn't like and the parts I'd probably excel at. (She was right on all counts.) I appreciated her unvarnished opinion and her willingness to tell me the good, the bad, and the ugly. I trusted Stacy because she was a straight shooter and would not suggest I take a job that wasn't a good fit or wouldn't serve my interests. If I couldn't hack the undercover lifestyle and unconventional job requirements, she'd let me know.

I was a lot like Stacy, so if she could do it, then I probably could, too. I reasoned that her success boded well for me. This was when I realized that comparison can be a beautiful thing. When we see people who look or act like us achieve something admirable, we realize, consciously or subconsciously, *If they can do it, there's no reason I shouldn't give it a try.* We need to be able to see ourselves in people farther ahead on the journey to know that we, too, are just as capable.

CHAPTER FIVE
UNCERTAINTY

Two roads diverged in a wood, and I—
I took the one less traveled by,
And that has made all the difference.

—Robert Frost, "The Road Not Taken"

I have received many messages from people who have read my memoir *Breaking Cover: My Secret Life in the CIA and What It Taught Me about What's Worth Fighting For*, or listened to one of my keynote presentations. They frequently say, "You've inspired me to get off the X, but now I'd like to know, how do I do that?" Or desperate seekers ask, "How do I figure out what I'm supposed to be doing?"

As you'll notice in these questions, uncertainty can bind you to the X in two different ways: first, as you try to solve the mystery of what your goal or objective should be, and second, when you know what that goal is but are unsure how to bring it to fruition.

Uncertainty in both of these forms is a D&D campaign that strongly suggests not moving forward until you figure out *exactly* what you want or you know *for sure* which option will work. Adhering to this mental approach is like problem-solving in a void. If you leave the question to ricochet in your mind, you will drown in doubt and anxiety.

A theoretical approach to the questions about your future will never work. Instead, what's required is a kinetic approach. You must investigate the options incessantly. You must beat the streets like an operative in training and keep trying, keep exploring, and keep moving until you stumble onto that yellow brick road.

ALL HAIL THE LATE BLOOMERS

Probably the most frustrated I have ever been in my life was in my early twenties while trying to figure out the career for which I was best suited. I wasn't one of those lucky people who knew from an early age what she wanted to be. Instead, I found myself a newly graduated, newly married, and newly transplanted resident of Washington, DC, lost in a sea of extremely smart and sophisticated people. It seemed like everyone had a career plan and was off to the races, while I was stuck at the gate.

I remember asking everyone I met whose job seemed even mildly interesting, "How did you get here? What did you study? Do you like it? What does it take to do this job well?" I peppered people with these and a hundred other probing questions, mining their backgrounds and skill sets for clues to my own future.

When I worked as an administrative assistant at an international relief and development organization, I explored public health degrees, international development careers, lobbying and advocacy jobs, proposal writing jobs, and Capitol Hill staffer positions. It never seemed as if I had the requisite knowledge or expertise.

For years I searched while my friends kicked off illustrious careers left and right. Looking at the difference between my career progression and everyone else's left me pondering, *What's wrong with me? Why can't I find my way?* All the rejections seemed to indicate I wasn't smart enough or experienced enough. Add to that my general lack of interest in any of the jobs I had learned about, and I thought I must be missing the boat or doing something terribly wrong.

All the resumes I submitted and the resulting chorus of cricket chirping was gut-wrenching. Some days I felt as if other people were doing amazing things, and I'd have to resign myself to a life of mediocrity.

But the truth of the matter was that I was a late bloomer. This category is the opposite of the much-celebrated wunderkind: the early achiever. People like me don't rise quickly, score the highest on the SAT, or get recruited straight out of college into the elite strata of the workforce. We develop at a different pace.

Rich Karlgaard, former publisher of *Forbes* magazine, shed a powerful light on our culture's obsession with early achievement in his book *Late Bloomers: The Power of Patience in a World Obsessed with Early Achievement.* "Obsession with early achievement creates a strong expectation that young people should be achieving more, achieving it faster, and achieving it younger," he wrote. "For the twenty-somethings among us, the message is clear: Succeed right now or you never will."[6]

And this cultural expectation isn't levied just on young people; it's an assumption about progress that's thrust at us at every age. If we allow the fallacy of "achieve quickly or not at all" to color our self-assessments, we might give up trying. As a young adult I was about to resign myself to settling on the X before I even got started. Buying into the myth that talent is tied to early achievement can cause depression and anxiety for those who don't measure up to these expectations. We all have a purpose, but the ways in which we develop and our timetables for that development can be quite different.

Some of us need time to percolate. Since I wasn't preened in my developmental years to understand foreign affairs nor raised in a family that discussed politics, I needed time to develop a solid understanding of our nation's institutions. I needed to learn the

ABCs of Capitol Hill and the dynamics that drive policymaking and change. I needed to observe how the branches of government interact with one another and the ways in which nongovernmental entities influence government actors. I needed to comprehend these power dynamics and how to successfully lobby issues by finding ways to connect and communicate with stakeholders.

Exposure to the odd landscape of competing interests and personalities would be crucial to my development as an intelligence officer and then later as an international corporate consultant and human rights advocate. My pace of development was different. I would need a ridiculously deep understanding of government systems and diplomacy when Joseph and I took on the challenge of assisting Iraqis uprooted by ISIS, as well as other human rights cases where lives were at stake.*

Please don't let your uncertainty overwhelm you. You can gain clarity of direction and discover angles to help push yourself off the X. Most importantly, realize that you're not alone. Though it may look as though everyone else has it all figured out, there are probably more slow starters than you realize, and people whose paths look more like those of whirling dervishes than Olympic sprinters.

BILL'S STORY: UNCERTAINTY IN THE CROSSHAIRS

The recipe for a great career doesn't usually include taking the helm of a dying company, especially if you've never cared to become a CEO.

My friend Bill Yeargin desired to use his limited corporate experience as a consultant in the maritime industry. As he prepared to launch his consulting career, he was offered the position

---

*See chapter 12 in this book and chapters 16–20 of my first book, *Breaking Cover*, for more information on this exciting post-CIA operation.

as president and CEO of Correct Craft, a boat design and manufacturing company. Bill was not interested in the position, and so he politely declined.

About a year later, after the fourth CEO had walked away from the company, the board of directors made Bill a second offer. They really wanted him to try to turn the company around. A turnaround was indeed needed: Correct Craft had seen four CEOs in four years and had a track record that would suggest a highly problematic business model, a toxic culture, and an untold number of internal problems.

In addition to these concerns, Bill explained to me that had numerous personal reasons to say no to the opportunity. He lived in West Palm Beach, Florida, and his family's commitments firmly tied them practically, financially, and emotionally to the area. Moving to the company's Orlando headquarters, even in the best of circumstances, seemed an unrealistic and unnecessarily stressful proposition. And this was not the best of circumstances. Would it even be possible to turn things around at a company when so many others had failed? Uncertainty ruled the day.

For some reason, though, Bill was intrigued. So he started small, simply exploring how difficult it would be to move his family from South to Central Florida. Incredibly, the obstacles that had loomed so large were resolved with minimal effort. The quick dissolution of those barriers meant that *they* were not a reason to reject the opportunity. Bill took these unexpected breakthroughs as a sign that maybe he should accept this difficult mission. The "What should I do?" uncertainty seemed to have been answered. Now to address the key question, "How do I do this?"

Expectations were low. No one believed that Bill (or really anyone) could be successful in turning things around at Correct Craft. But instead of being overwhelmed by the enormity of the challenge, Bill reasoned that he couldn't make things worse. With that frame of mind, he deleted "fear of failure" from his computations and stepped in as president and CEO of Correct Craft in September 2006.

Bill approached his mission in the same way he had recently completed a marathon. At the last half mile of the race with the finish line in sight, when he felt as though he could not go on, Bill did what Bill always does: he focused on one step at a time. "Right foot. Left foot. Right foot . . ." Thus, Bill got off the X. Focusing on the next step helped block the pain and uncertainty of a weary mind and body. He willed himself across the finish line.

Bill refused to be caught in the crosshairs of uncertainty in his new role, too. Instead of being overwhelmed by all that needed to be done, he focused on one doable step at a time. Bill's operational priorities were to assemble the right team and address company culture by focusing on staff development. This modest approach eventually resulted in the absolute turnaround of Correct Craft.

Not only did the company not die, but it expanded into a global enterprise. The Florida-based corporation now encompasses a large family of marine crafts and technologies, including the Nautique and Centurion boat companies. Since Bill took this crazy career gamble, Correct Craft's revenue has increased from $40 million to over $1 billion.[7]

Bill is grateful he didn't permit the waves of uncertainty to cloud his judgment and keep him from an opportunity to develop as a leader. Neither should you let uncertainty stop you any longer. Your best life might be waiting just around that corner.

CHAPTER SIX
FEAR

Thinking will not overcome fear, but action will.

—William Clement Stone, *The Success System That Never Fails*

Fear is a powerful motivator. Its most basic function is to set off alarm bells when we're in physical danger. But when fear becomes the basis of nonemergency decision-making, it can cause us to shrink away from platforms of opportunity. Why is that? Fear in motion, aka worry, is very needy. It demands our attention, depleting our physiological resources. When that happens, we lack the energy required to do anything besides survive.

Fear is an internal D&D campaign that weakens our focus and resolve. When we allow fear to take the reins, we shrink back. We settle for paths that seem more doable. We choose to engage in activities that don't result in heart palpitations.

Allowing fear to govern our choices magnifies our vulnerabilities against a bevy of imagined failures or disasters. Yet most of the time the things we worry about don't come true. So why do we capitulate to our fear?

I have met thousands of people at my speaking events who said they would love to be an undercover spy jetting around the world, but they're too scared. I laugh and then tell them the truth: I was scared, too. But I did it anyway.

Not everyone is cut out to be a spy, but is it possible that you have been overselling your fear and underselling yourself in the process?

NERINA'S STORY, PART 1: TAKE THE WHEEL

When my cousin Nerina got married, I was living abroad. As with most family milestones, I missed out on meeting her boyfriend, watching the relationship grow, and attending the wedding. Therefore, I didn't know Nerina was having second thoughts about her decision to marry Martin. I didn't know she was struggling. I had assumed that this was a joyful event. But she hid from her closest family and friends the shocking realization that she'd rushed into something that wasn't good for her.

On the night of her wedding, while her new husband was sleeping, Nerina lay in bed crying, overwhelmed by a gut feeling that she'd just made one of the worst decisions of her life. And for reasons she couldn't explain, the following thought pierced her brain: *Now my life is going to be so hard.*

Indeed, this marriage was not a wise decision. Her new husband demonstrated narcissistic traits, pushing hard for Nerina's attention and for control over her life and relationships. His efforts to isolate her kicked in soon after the wedding. He seemed jealous of anyone who spent time with her and did his best to pull her away from her network of family and friends. Nerina loved her sons from her first marriage more than life itself, so the mother-child bonds became a dysfunctional point of contention with her new husband.

Things went from bad to worse five years later when Nerina unexpectedly got pregnant at age thirty-nine. That's when she felt completely trapped—stuck in a toxic relationship and unsure how to get out of it. Her career as a massage therapist didn't pay enough for Nerina to live on her own, so the trapped feeling continued to grow, along with her swelling tummy.

Nerina also felt stagnant in her career, no longer challenged as a massage therapist. Something was missing. She loved learning about anatomy and the human body, but she wasn't using this knowledge in a way that fulfilled her. When people asked what she did for a living, she'd respond, "I'm *just* a massage therapist." Her own words betrayed her disappointment with her station in life.

One day the doctor she worked with planted a seed when he said, "You know, Nerina, you would make such a great nurse." He recognized that she connected quickly and easily with her clients and treated them with empathy and compassion. As a result, many of them chose to remain with her for years of treatment.

The doctor's comment about nursing intrigued her. But laid against the fact that she was having a baby, the idea of becoming a nurse sounded ridiculous. She was almost forty years old. What kind of madness suggested she could go back to school and start over again with a new baby in tow? Nerina had never even liked school.

Yet every moment with her husband seemed to get harder and more dysfunctional. She had to do something. She had to plot a way forward. She didn't want to depend on another person to put a roof over her head or food on the table. Her financial dependency had placed her in a vulnerable position, and she wanted to take back control of her life.

As Nerina considered her options, she saw a meme on social media that hit her like a ton of bricks: "You're scared to take a four-year course because you're thirty-two, because by the time you're done, you'll be thirty-six. But whether you take the course or not, in four years you'll still be thirty-six." (In Nerina's case, she'd be forty-four.) She reasoned that she'd either sacrifice to get where she needed to go or remain hopelessly stuck on the X.

Nerina gathered the courage to make the bold decision. She was going to do whatever it took; she was going to study to become a nurse. All the unknowns terrified her: What if she couldn't pass chemistry or microbiology? What if she did all of this work and couldn't get into nursing school? Or what if she successfully made it through nursing school but then couldn't pass the board exams? The fear was tremendous, but the fear of failure was even worse.

To juggle the demands of being a mother to a newborn, a preteen, and a teenager, Nerina went into what she called "survival mode." She told herself, *You have to get through school no matter what it requires. You have to learn to focus because your survival is based on how well you do that. Don't look left. Don't look right. And don't look back.*

Nerina learned to make the most of every waking moment. She was laser focused on the tasks in front of her. Every minute mattered. She had to remind herself repeatedly that this season of crazed busyness and exhaustion would not last forever. She would come out on the other end better, more capable, and, most importantly, independent.

NERINA'S STORY, PART 2: REFRAME FOR THE WIN

Nerina had grown up interpreting fear as an indicator of things to avoid. But now she realized she couldn't get unstuck and move forward without busting through that fear. She was beginning to realize that giving in to fear was unhealthy. It was holding her back. That darn fear got in the way of everything. To beat it she had to reframe what she was telling herself about the decisions she was making. She decided to flip the conversations in her head.

For example, Nerina stressed over her lack of options due to her inability to support herself and thus leave the marriage. Desperation now motivated her to flip that script and remind herself that she was *creating* options by working hard. No matter how tired or worn out she felt, she told herself that this wouldn't last forever. She could endure the pain now for the peace later.

Nerina's next big thought obstacle was her age. She was older than most students in the program by decades. Why did she think this was bad? Why did she assume that because she wasn't typical, she was at a disadvantage? Nerina realized this fallacy and flipped it to remind herself that one of her greatest advantages was the life experience she brought into the classroom—the twenty years she'd worked on the human body as a therapist treating various conditions. She rejected the self-defeating statement, "I can't do this because I will be forty-four years old in four years." She reframed it into the supportive and empowering statement, "In four years I will be forty-four, and I will be a nurse!"

One final thought obstacle was the concern Nerina had with her ability to study. She challenged herself to consider the fact that she could learn—she'd been learning about the human body for decades. And she wanted to know more. She was hungry to understand and passionate about building her expertise. Her fascination with health and wellness and the human body would drive her to figure out how to use flash cards, join study groups, find skills-based videos on YouTube, and invest in test-preparation materials.

As Nerina began her program of study attacking the necessary prerequisites, our ninety-two-year-old grandmother entered a period of physical decline. She kept falling or getting infections, which landed her in the hospital for days at a time. Then after a particularly wonderful visit with extended family members, Grandma declared with great joy, "If I died tomorrow, I would be perfectly happy."

Ironically, that night she went to sleep and never woke up. As she lay there unconscious, her systems slowly shut down. Julie, my cousin Jenna, Nerina, my aunt Mary, my niece Danielle, and my aunt's husband, Steve, gathered around her bed in a vigil that we thought would last a day or two. Instead, our sweet Italian grandma kept going and going. Her small body was much stronger than any of us knew.

Hospice nurses coached Nerina on the dying process so she would understand what was happening. As Grandma's petite body went through the excruciating process of shutting down, each of us wordlessly took a role in some dimension of her care. Mary and I played gospel music, prayed for her, and read from her favorite book, the Bible. Nerina, Jenna, and Danielle took on roles I and others in the family couldn't do, such as tending to aspects of physical care such as clearing her mouth, administering morphine, and taking her temperature.

It was during this period of time that Nerina realized that she was, indeed, called to nursing. During the five long days and nights when we rarely left Grandma's side, we were exhausted, strung out, and sometimes delirious from lack of sleep. It was terrible and it was beautiful. It was challenging beyond measure, but it was sacred.

No matter how hard it got listening to the labored breathing or the "death rattle" of secretions in Grandma's lungs, we were motivated to be there, to cheer her to the other side. Then, at 5:43 a.m. on January 28, Grandma's spirit finally released from her body, not slowly or peacefully but like a rocket shot into heaven. We erupted into shouts of joy. "You did it, Grandma! You did it!"

Nerina discovered real purpose in doing difficult things that others (like me) couldn't do. That's something you can't ignore. Grandma in her passing—God Almighty in his providence—confirmed Nerina's calling. This knowledge was integral to the strength she would need to sustain her over the next four years.

With a dedication that stunned us all, Nerina worked her way through every obstacle during that manic time: She completed her prerequisites. She obtained her associate's degree. She applied and was accepted to nursing school. She labored long and hard through labs, exams, research, writing, and hundreds of hours of study. Meanwhile, she shuffled the competing demands of being a mother, wife, and student.

But all the sacrifice was worth it: Nerina successfully graduated from nursing school in December 2021. A month later she passed the dreaded nursing boards with flying colors. Nerina achieved what she once thought impossible: she became a bona fide nurse working first in the cardiology unit and then in the labor-and-delivery unit of a well-respected hospital. When she gets onto the elevator and presses the button to go up to her floor, she can't help but break into a huge grin. She can hardly believe where she is standing. She is so proud of the nursing badge she sports, a badge of honor that reminds her how far she's come. She loves her job, loves the team she works with, and loves her new life.

Nerina believes that she was more capable of achieving this goal in her forties than in her twenties. Life had gifted her the necessary experience, maturity, and urgency. And by the time she entered the nursing program, she had the grit needed to counteract feelings of not studying enough, not doing enough, or not being a good enough mother. Nerina wasn't late. She was perfectly prepared.

As a result of these remarkable achievements, she extracted herself from her toxic marital relationship and now fully supports herself and her family, pays her bills, and saves for the future. She has a whole new level of confidence and the knowledge that she's capable of so much more than she originally believed. And, just as importantly, she has modeled to her children what it looks like to sacrifice to get ahead, work hard, and reap the benefits of that dedicated labor.

It's never too late to move yourself forward. What reframing do you need to do to focus on your next step?

THE NECESSITY OF FOCUS

Being able to focus when you are a ball of nerves is an essential skill for living your best life. Like Nerina, I learned how critical focus was to gaining mastery over my nerves. If you can't operate around those nerves, you can't succeed in the clandestine service. Intelligence officers are constantly mitigating risk, but you can't mitigate risk if you are overcome by fear or anxiety.

That is why the CIA offer of employment is conditional on your ability to pass the tradecraft training course. This yearlong training teaches you the ins and outs of espionage and weeds out those who don't have an operational mindset, those who can't handle huge amounts of stress, and those who lack the personality required to live and operate in a foreign country. Throughout training, you must demonstrate an ability to operate under the gun in a calm and collected manner, even if it feels as though your insides are exploding. Thankfully, they gave us plenty of chances to master the art of focus in a wide variety of simulations mimicking everything from regular operations to life-and-death situations.

One of the first sets of skills we were taught was surveillance detection. Intelligence officers must know whether they are being followed, because the worst possible thing you can do is be followed to a meeting with a secret source, thereby revealing the identity of your source. If a foreign intelligence officer follows you to the meeting, this could result in your source's detainment or possibly death, depending on where you are in the world. A brutal reality.

The CIA begins with this section of training probably because the implications of doing it wrong are so vast, and if you can't take the heat, you might as well figure it out sooner rather than later. I'd be lying if I said I wasn't scared to try my hand at this. I was. Could I do it? I didn't know. I'd never cased a joint to rob it or shoplift. I'd never stalked or clandestinely followed someone. I had no basis upon which to be confident of my ability to conduct surveillance or figure out whether I was under surveillance. But I chose to not dwell on what *could happen* and focus on learning the skill itself.

On the day I was scheduled to kick off on my first vehicular surveillance detection route (SDR), I was a ball of nerves. As I sat in my vehicle, my stomach churned. *Oh no, don't do that. Focus, Michele*, I told myself.

I carefully adjusted the mirrors to be sure I had the best possible view of the cars behind and beside me. My shaking hands placed the tiny notebook on my right thigh, which I'd use to scribble down license plate numbers and the makes and models of cars that I thought might be following me during the two-hour SDR.

The route I created was carefully mapped out. Plus, I had driven it at least three times to ensure I had the route memorized. If you get lost in the middle of an SDR or even take a wrong turn, it could mean failing the exercise. On top of that, the route had to be exact in terms of timing. I had a window of just a few minutes to arrive at my final destination.

There were so many things to think about and so many things that could go wrong. Students had to remember every turn in the two-hour drive and take stock of every suspicious vehicle. If possible, we tried to get a description of vehicle occupants when we thought we had surveillance. All the while we were trying to drive safely, not hit anyone, follow the law, and mind the clock to ensure the precise timing of each leg, each vehicle stop, and arrival at our destinations. So, basically, we had to remember everything!

As I waited nervously for my kickoff time to arrive, I was perspiring but doing my best to take deep breaths to calm down. Every now and then, a panicked thought would ricochet through my mind. *What in the name of God am I doing? What if I take a wrong turn? What if I miss my window?* This is what fear feels like: panic at the starting line thinking about all that could go wrong.

Then I had to take those thoughts captive and remind myself that every other student had to be feeling the same way. Most of us were intimidated by the new skill set we had to master. I could not let my brain hold me back. To remain focused, I decided to reject the fear of failure and concentrate not on everything I had to remember but on the one thing right in front of my face: pushing off to begin my SDR at the right time. I had to jettison all other distractions.

Some people couldn't take the stress and dropped out of the training program in the first few months. I decided not to. I moved forward in spite of the fear. Much like Nerina, I felt as though I had to succeed because no other job opportunities had come through after I graduated from Georgetown. I had applied to dozens of other positions, and this was the only job offer I got. Throughout training, I kept thinking, *You have to succeed. There's no option B.*

In the course of pushing myself forward, I learned that I *could* identify surveillance. It wasn't my favorite thing in the world, but I could do it. I had been forced to learn the makes and models of cars, and the patterns of their respective headlights at night, and I had become proficient in reading license plates. I learned to drive with my eyes constantly darting to the rearview and side-view mirrors to log potential surveillants. I passed the surveillance portion of the course with an enormous sense of relief.

With each new skill set I acquired, the fear that had dominated my vision was now withdrawing into the background. The discipline I practiced—of focusing on what I *could* control—would serve me well throughout training and in my career. You have to keep the negative, self-defeating thoughts at bay. Focus on each little step required to move in the right direction.

MISSION PLANNING: GAIN MASTERY OVER FEAR AND ANXIETY

Operational planning in the CIA is designed to bring your thoughts into alignment and help you focus on the right things at the right time. Here's how the mission planning process works:

1. *Design your operation.* First, you lay out the steps necessary to achieve a particular set of objectives.

2. *Anticipate Murphy.* One of the many CIA mantras regarding the challenges of executing operations in the real world is recognizing Murphy's Law: anything that can go wrong will go wrong. The integration of Murphy's Law into the operational-planning process is a constant reminder not to hide behind risk or try to pretend it's not there. You plan for Murphy. You anticipate potential difficulties. You look problems in the face, and you call them out. You list everything that could possibly go awry during a mission.

3. *Plan responses to the what-ifs.* Once you lay out all the unanticipated events that could interrupt and threaten the integrity of the operation, you plan appropriate responses to each of the *what-ifs*. What if A happens? Then I'll respond by doing B, C, or D. It's helpful to carry out this exercise with other experienced officers who can help you consider physical, environmental, cultural, political, or even social challenges you hadn't conceived of.

   This is a fascinating process because it empowers you to manage inherent operational risks. This is critical, because you can either focus on fear or focus on your goal. Your brain cannot do both at the same time. You have to prepare for the operation by thinking of all the things that could go wrong so you can plan for and mitigate those risks. This prepares you to respond appropriately to curveballs if or when they present themselves. There is a science to all of this: when your brain feels more in control, it calms the amygdala and its associated stress response.

4. *Focus your mind, leave the planning behind.* Now that you have thoroughly planned for your mission, know all the steps you must take, and have planned for possible contingencies, what comes next is simple, yet profound:

> leave it all behind. You have to transition your focus from the wide view to the narrow mechanics of your operation as it unfolds.

The moment you begin your mission is not the time to regurgitate all the ways Murphy might show up. You already did that, and you planned for it. Now you have to focus on each step in front of you. Because every moment matters, you must be all in. You must be fully present and aware of your surroundings so you don't miss an indicator that something is awry.

Human intelligence (HUMINT) operations require your full attention. When you kick off, you train your brain to focus on each portion of the mission as it unfolds: you execute a well-conceived SDR, collect the intelligence, then return safely to base. You must stay in the moment, maintaining a laser focus just as elite athletes do: swimmers who mind each stroke, Formula 1 drivers who concentrate on each curve of the track, and gymnasts who fix their minds on each tumbling pass.

The more you train your brain to focus, the better you will be at filtering extraneous information and removing distractions. Many people who are frozen on the X have considered Murphy and then allowed the fear of Murphy to take control. They obsess over the problem instead of focusing on potential solutions. Getting off the X requires moving from step 2 to step 3 and onward, empowering yourself to move past Murphy's emotional manipulations. Fear and anxiety are not the last word; they are merely thought obstacles on your path to purpose and success.

Studies show that as you focus on action versus the content of your feelings, the neural networks of your brain change. You literally rewire the thought patterns of your brain, which leads to a reduction of anxiety and its impact on your life. You can, in fact, train your brain, which makes it progressively easier to move yourself forward and achieve your goals.[8]

CHAPTER SEVEN
CIRCUMSTANCES

I determined I would not be crushed.

—Elizabeth Packard, quoted by Kate Moore in *The Woman They Could Not Silence*

One category can land you on the X that has nothing to do with self-limiting thought obstacles. I'm talking about foundation-shifting events with the capacity to alter the pace, focus, and trajectory of your life. These circumstances include but are not limited to job loss, marital problems, divorce, illness or disease, death of a loved one, loss of your home, pandemics, legal issues, war and conflict, and political or religious persecution.

In other words, you suddenly become a member of a club that you never wanted to join.

When circumstances beyond your control profoundly disrupt your life, the internal D&D campaign tells you that you may never recover. It threatens you with permanency—the inability to ever get past the tragedy or injustice. The pain is so profound you can't imagine feeling anything else. You question whether you have the capacity to survive.

With twists and turns that are out of your control, getting off the X becomes profoundly difficult. Run if you can, walk if you are able, but if crawling off the X is all you are capable of, then that's what you must do.

LISA'S STORY: DEAD ON ARRIVAL

Her consciousness fought against a thick blanket of grogginess and exhaustion. As Lisa came to, pain overwhelmed every square inch of her body: stabbing pain, aching pain, and waves of pain. Suddenly aware of the cacophony of beeps and whirls around her, the twenty-two-year-old wondered where she was. Her eyes flickered open, revealing a jumble of wires and tubes hooked up to various parts of her body. She was covered in bandages, medical tape, patches, and monitors. Every time she tried to move, it felt as though she were underwater fighting a strong current. She must have been thinking at the very least, *Where am I and what is happening?*

As the terror inside her grew, Lisa moved her head to the side. Beside her sat a kind-looking man. She thought he looked trustworthy, so she cried to him for help: "Please, they're trying to kill me!" At the same time, she worked to loosen herself from the network of tubes and wires restraining her.

In response to her screams and the pandemonium of the alarms attached to the wires she had disengaged, strange people rushed into the room. They seemed to be working against her, trying to prevent her from getting away. She looked back to the nice man, who she later would learn was her father, hoping he would help. Then just as suddenly as she woke up, everything went black.

Two weeks prior to this, Lisa was headed to the local Winn-Dixie grocery store to submit her two-week notice. It was Labor Day 1995. She had just received a scholarship to help cover her living expenses so she could stop working full-time, concentrate on nursing school, and spend more time with her one-year-old son.

Lisa's grandmother arrived at her house. They had planned to go shopping at the mall after her quick trip to Winn-Dixie. Lisa had already installed her son's car seat and placed the diaper bag in the truck, but Lisa's grandmother decided at the last minute to stay home with the baby so Lisa didn't have to rush her meeting. Lisa agreed to pick them up after she finished with her supervisor. Lisa's sister, Carolyn, was also at the house.

After handing in her resignation and planning her final work schedule, Lisa left Winn-Dixie to return home. Just a few miles from her house in Astatula, Florida, a drunk driver ran a stop sign, T-boning Lisa's 1984 Ford F-150. She never saw it coming. The impact was so severe the truck split in two, separating the cab of the truck from the bed. The tremendous force caused Lisa's body to slip out of her seat belt; she was then ejected through the windshield. Both Lisa and the cab of the truck skidded away from the initial point of impact, coming to rest half a mile down County Road 561. Lisa's motionless body lay a few feet from the battered front half of the vehicle.

A family friend driving by the accident recognized the "Natural Blonde" personalized license plate still attached to the front of the truck. He quickly headed to the family's house to notify them. After hearing the terrible news, Carolyn grabbed her nephew, put him in her truck, and headed to the accident site with her grandmother in tow. They arrived at the scene just as a blanket was being placed over Lisa's mangled body.

Police officers stopped Carolyn and asked who she was. When they found out she was the victim's sister, they notified her that they were looking for the small child who would have been riding in the car seat. Diapers were scattered all over the ground, as were empty beer bottles from the perpetrator's vehicle. Nodding to the baby on her hip, Carolyn answered with great relief, "This is the baby you're looking for. The baby wasn't in the truck, he was with us."

Lisa's body was airlifted to the trauma unit at Orlando Regional Medical Center. She was classified as DOA—dead on arrival. Hearing that the victim's family had arrived and were waiting anxiously for news, the doctor decided to go to the waiting room to notify them that Lisa had passed away. As he began to walk away from Lisa's lifeless body, something grabbed his attention: the readings on the monitor changed from a flat line to a faint blip, indicating that Lisa was not dead after all, or had been dead but was now alive. Instead of being moved to the morgue, she was kept in the trauma unit hooked up to various life-support systems.

The doctor told Lisa's parents to contact family and friends so they could say their goodbyes. Given that she'd already been declared dead once, he knew Lisa probably would not make it through the night. She had suffered a severe brain injury (her brain was swollen and bleeding), a skull fracture, a ruptured ear drum that was leaking spinal fluid, hematomas on her head and right hip, broken ribs that punctured both lungs, a broken sternum, a ruptured spleen, a tilted hip from slipping out of the seat belt, and significant loss of skin. Pieces of asphalt from County Road 561 were embedded in Lisa's skin and protruding from her left foot. In addition, several discs in her spine had shattered, penetrating her nerves. In the process of sliding down the road, all her clothes were torn off and her skin was shredded like hamburger meat. The only part of Lisa's body that remained intact was her face.

Somehow, Lisa did not die that night. Three of the other young people brought into the ER that fateful evening passed away. As grief erupted in the waiting room, all Lisa's parents could do was hope and pray. The next day they were surprised that Lisa was still alive, but she was in a coma. They were told she would probably never wake up.

Lisa's condition was hit or miss for several weeks, but against all odds she emerged from the coma. When she regained consciousness for the second time, she saw a sign on the hospital door that read "Jane Doe," the original placard placed there when she was flown to the trauma unit before the hospital received her ID.

A sweet-looking lady sat in a chair beside her bed. Lisa looked at her and asked, "Is that my name? Am I Jane?" The lady's eyes filled with tears. She stood up, walked over, and calmly replied, "No, that's not your name. Your name is Lisa Lynne Marcum, and I'm your mom."

Her mother? Lisa had no recollection of this woman. And even more puzzling to those in the room was her repeated question, "Who am I again?"

Lisa's survival was a miracle, but her body was a complete mess. And worse, her brain was unalterably damaged, the accident having erased the knowledge of her own identity. Lisa had profound or severe retrograde amnesia, which is the loss of memory acquired before an injury. Her condition was so extreme she lost all access to autobiographical information as well as general world knowledge.

In other words, Lisa had no idea who the one-year-old blond, blue-eyed child was, the baby she had conceived, birthed, and raised for the past year of his life. For that matter, Lisa didn't even know how babies were made, such was the severity of her brain damage. This type of memory loss caused by traumatic brain injury is usually temporary. In Lisa's case, it was permanent.

At age twenty-two, Lisa had to start at the beginning. After coming off life support, she faced a long recovery process from extensive physical injuries as well as the trauma of knowing nothing about herself or her family. Lisa was a stranger in her own life. Imagine being dropped into another person's skin and having to learn everything about her from scratch. She had to meet and develop a new knowledge of her parents, siblings, grandparents, child, ex-husband, and everyone else she once knew.

In addition to those profound relational losses, Lisa also lost her knowledge of basic skills. She had to learn how to walk, talk, eat, dress, bathe, and write her name. Lisa's brain damage was so extensive that when asked by a therapist who the president of the United States was, she replied, "What's a president?"

She didn't know what had once been her own unique strengths, weaknesses, talents, or skills. She didn't even remember what foods she liked. Her family cared for Lisa and her son until she relearned the basics of life. She had to raise herself up first, then learn how to raise a child.

Lisa never regained any of her memory. To this day, she doesn't know anything about herself or what the world was like prior to her accident. She has no memory of what it's like to be a child or a teenager. Her type of amnesia is among the rarest of all forms of memory loss. Few people in the world have sustained injuries like Lisa's and lived to talk about it.

If anyone has found herself on one of the worst Xs of life, it was Lisa. She endured the ultimate unexpected ambush by a selfish drunk driver whose actions stole the first twenty-two years of her life. To add insult to injury, the driver was never charged for drunk driving; he received only a minor moving violation. As a result, Lisa never received a dime from him for her injuries, which still require major medical interventions and surgery.

Lisa was thrown squarely onto the X by circumstances over which she had no control. I wouldn't blame her if she were deeply traumatized and barely able to function. But no, not Lisa. She is one of the most loving and encouraging people I have ever known, exuding joy and selflessness. When any of our friends needs encouragement, Lisa is the first to say, "You can do it!"

Lisa's family was told she wouldn't live through the night, but she survived. They were told she probably wouldn't emerge from the coma, and yet two weeks later she woke up. They were told she would never walk again. Less than a year later, she was walking without assistance. Her family was told that if she survived, she wouldn't be able to function very well, but if you saw her today, you wouldn't have a clue what she's been through. They said she would need a guardian for the rest of her life to handle her affairs. A year later she was permitted to take control of her own life. They said she would never be able to break free from the chains of all the misery inflicted on her, but as she explains, "It's been more than twenty-five years, and I've broken free from not only this tragic event but others that have come after it."

Lisa is the ultimate champion in getting off the X. She was determined not to allow doctors, therapists, or injuries to dictate what she could and could not do. She is a walking miracle.

Any time I face a challenge, I think of Lisa and my "challenges" are put into proper context. Does that mean Lisa doesn't struggle? Far from it. Decades after the accident, Lisa still suffers from a wide range of physical ailments related to her injuries. She still bears physical scars and sees a host of doctors to manage the evolving requirements of a body so battered.

Yet Lisa has never allowed herself to wallow in self-pity. Instead, she focuses on all she has gained: her life. She has a deep love and appreciation for her family, her children, and the life she now lives. She is grateful to God that she was given another chance. Lisa is an incredible example of what's possible when you give yourself to a force much greater than you, who can give purpose and meaning to suffering.

Lisa is on a mission to use her story to reach others who don't know whether it's possible to move forward. The bottom line is that you may not be able to do it alone. You may need to rely on the love and support of family and friends to get you through the worst moments, the times when you can't help yourself. The times when you can't get off the floor. The times when you need someone to drop everything and come to your aid, pray with you, hold you, cry with you, and lift you up with words of encouragement.

If Lisa can rise from such life-altering circumstances and get off the X, there's hope for all of us. And it may take crawling to get off the X, but if that's all you can do, that's exactly where you start.

NOT THE LAST WORD

At numerous times in our lives, we might think that some awful circumstance has wedded us to a suboptimal life, or that events beyond our control have plotted our future. As we now know, Lisa's devastating accident didn't have to dictate everything that came next. Though in the moment it feels as though there's no way to recover from the heartbreak or massive setbacks, these circumstances don't need to hijack your internal response or even set the tone for your future.

The benefit of hindsight is realizing that these things are not as set in stone as we might imagine. When the CIA withdrew its offer of an analyst position (more on that in chapter 19), the rejection I received included the following language: "There is no appeal of this decision." But this was not the last word. I *did* get into the CIA; I just entered through another door and was re-recruited into a position that better suited me. I was also told by CIA physicians that because of my autoimmune disease (ulcerative colitis), I would never be permitted to serve in a field position. I then spent the next ten years doing mostly that: serving in the field.

Just because you are told you can't do something or won't be permitted to do so, don't assume it's the last word. Circumstances change. You might learn of loopholes and options you hadn't been aware of. And of course, as in Lisa's case, miracles do happen. What I now understand is that I must do my best to moderate my emotional reactions to setbacks or even catastrophic circumstances, because they are never the last word if I don't give them that space. Kowtowing to circumstances can kill you. Believing for better may save your life and catapult you into a better destiny. Whatever landed you on the X does not have to keep you there.

PART 3: TRADECRAFT

The spy who does not take tradecraft seriously is unlikely to remain a spy for very long.

—H. H. A. Cooper and Lawrence J. Redlinger, *Making Spies: A Talent Spotter's Handbook*

The ability to execute successful operations is contingent on the application of good tradecraft, the tactics, techniques, and procedures (TTPs) used to plan and execute intelligence activities safely and effectively. The use of sound tradecraft enables officers to manage and mitigate risk. A range of tradecraft methodologies can be used to achieve different objectives, depending on the nature of the target and the officer's unique operational environment.

CHAPTER EIGHT
YOUR MISSION

I never did anything worth doing by accident. No, when I have fully decided that a result is worth getting, I go about it, and make trial after trial, until it comes.

—Thomas Edison

The enemy knows you are there, somewhere in the area. But you still need to make your mark. Setting up a meeting with your source is mission critical, because he's got the intelligence you need. Proper decisions can't be made without access to those secrets, so you run a carefully crafted three-hour surveillance detection route to be sure no one is following you. Everything hinges on your ability to move yourself forward in hostile territory.

After determining that you're clean, you ditch the vehicle and proceed on foot. It's dark, with only faint shadows cast by a nearby streetlamp as you approach the empty storefront. You enter a long corridor, a covered walkway between two buildings. As you move forward at a steady pace, you peer into the mirrored glass door at the end to catch a glimpse of potential surveillants. You've built numerous opportunities into this run to spot a tail. Thankfully, you spot only your reflection.

As you turn a corner, you reach into your coat pocket, pull out a small piece of white chalk, and drag it across the gray wall at hip level. This insignificant-looking mark on the wall will trigger a meeting with your secret source. It's been placed in the spot agreed to ahead of time, a location your source frequents. This scuff mark will be the positive indicator that he's being called to meet with you the following evening.

Twenty-five feet later, you emerge from the covered walkway into an alley. As you turn right onto the asphalt, a vehicle quietly pulls up to the side. You discreetly turn your head to ensure it's the right car. The window is down, and your CIA colleague is wearing her baseball cap—the go signal to let you know the coast is clear. You open the door and get into the car. She proceeds to the end of the alley and turns left onto the street as planned. Eventually, your colleague deposits you a block from your vehicle.

The next evening, after running another SDR, you arrive at the appointed pickup location within the six-minute window. You lean against the wall and wait in the shadows. Like clockwork, a vehicle pulls up, displaying the visual cue on the dashboard to indicate that the source is not being followed or under duress. The window comes down and your source issues the secret code words, just as you trained him. You return the appropriate verbal cue before climbing into the vehicle. That night you collect the vital intelligence you need from your source.

It's a tough environment, but you've carried out two significant operational acts using the tradecraft you were taught: the first to trigger the operation and the second to execute the clandestine meeting.

Intelligence officers can't wait for the perfect moment to act. We are always looking for ways to move our ops forward regardless of the danger or difficulty. It's the application of good tradecraft that equips us with the tools to advance your objectives. Hostile environment or not—we find ways to get the job done.

Your mission, should you choose to accept it, is to make the determination that you will not sit on that X any longer. You've wasted too much time waiting for the ideal set of circumstances, fretting about failure or letting fear dictate the way you move through life. Well, no more. Enough of those self-imposed guardrails. Your new mission is to use every tool at your disposal to push through intimidation, fear, uncertainty, and whatever else threatens your forward momentum.

Let's get on with it. Adventure awaits!

CHAPTER NINE
INERTIA BREAKERS

I don't see how he can ever finish, if he doesn't begin.

—Lewis Carroll, *Alice's Adventures in Wonderland*

When you are preparing to get off the X, it is useful to understand that the hardest part is getting started. Each time I launch a new project, whether big or small, it feels as if I am wearing lead shoes or trying to pull my leg out of quicksand. Summoning the mental and physical energy to take that first step seems to require a thermonuclear reaction to offset the inertia, to overcome the freeze response.

Since this is not an unusual predicament, it behooves us to understand what is happening in our brains. During an ambush, the freeze response is caused by shock. The human brain cannot make sense of the confusing events and struggles to process the peculiarity and enormity of what's happening. Overwhelmed by the strange inputs, the brain shuts down, rendering us unable to make rational decisions. We simply cannot move.

In life outside terrorist, criminal, or mass-casualty situations, we experience the freeze response for a similar reason: we have too many options. Psychologist Barry Schwartz described this phenomenon in his book *The Paradox of Choice: Why More Is Less*. "Though modern Americans have more choice than any group of people ever has had before, and thus, presumably, more freedom and autonomy," he explained, "we don't seem to be benefiting from it psychologically."[9]

In a nutshell, Schwartz has pointed out that having too many choices often overwhelms us, triggering feelings of helplessness, anxiety, and paralysis. Instead of empowering us, the multiplicity of options shuts down our brains. And maybe that's why it's gotten harder for millennials and members of Gen Z—the generations with the most access to free information—to chart their course. With such a deluge of options, how are they supposed to figure out what's next?

When researching our potential courses of action, we often fall through the rabbit hole of the internet universe. The tsunami of choices soon overwhelms us, and we don't know what to do or how to get started. We default to spending time on social media and enter the twilight zone of inactive bliss. That's why the first method of getting off the X is deceptively simple but supremely powerful: break the inertia of inaction, deconstruct the process of getting started.

BEHAVIORAL ACTIVATION: THE ONE THING

As Nerina considered going back to school at the age of forty, one particular obstacle loomed large in front of her: the financial-aid application form. She needed to determine whether she was eligible for educational grants or low-interest loans, yet every time Nerina thought about completing the form, it filled her with dread.

When she finally pushed herself forward and made herself fill out the form, she discovered two things. First of all, she didn't die. It wasn't a pleasant experience, but it was *not* life ending. Second, Nerina learned that this activity was worth every minute of her time, because she received an incredible amount of financial aid. It turns out this stumbling block was the one thing that enabled her to move forward with her studies unencumbered by worries of how she'd pay for her degree.

We all know logically that a form is not the scariest thing in the world. Nevertheless, this type of obstacle subconsciously represents the totality of unknowns we face when wanting to move forward. Intimidation, fear, or uncertainty warp our perceptions and cause us to view these obstacles as bigger and more formidable than they are. And even when we're dealing with legitimately scary circumstances, we cannot let disappointment, sadness, or grief hijack our decision-making process. Doing so would keep us wedded to the current predicament.

So how do we face these challenges?

Instead of waiting to feel better in order to act, what if you flipped the equation? What if you *acted* in order to feel better? This is referred to in cognitive behavioral therapy as "behavioral activation."

Behavioral activation is predicated on the notion that your behavior directly affects your mood, so action precedes emotion.[10] Researchers who focus on methodologies to alleviate negative emotions such as depression have found behavioral activation "on par with medication and slightly superior to cognitive therapy in the treatment of depression," because "behavioral activation shifts away from cognitions and feelings to focus on . . . behavior."[11]

If that is the case, instead of waiting to feel better or more motivated, consciously choose to do something . . . anything, no matter how big or small. The expenditure of energy will break the deep freeze. It will not only transform your mood, but it will generate a desire to do more. No matter how insignificant the action may seem, it taps into stores of motivation you didn't know you had. Moving is what causes you to move better because it sidesteps speculation, debate, and hesitancy.

Breaking self-defeating behavioral patterns that cause you to isolate yourself and avoid acting is the key to generating forward momentum. This simple methodology interrupts and thwarts the freeze response and ensures you don't get overwhelmed by the fifty possible actions required to get a new project off the ground. When you choose to do that *one thing*, it will have an impact on all the rest. And you do that every day until the project comes together. For me, it's not one and done. It's a decision I make almost every day when I'm uncertain or overwhelmed. It's what I do to unfreeze myself when I have a lot on my plate.

IMPERFECT STARTS AND OTHER JEDI MIND TRICKS

In one of my CIA tours, I was asked to take over the handling of a complicated case. The current operations officer was completing his tour and would be departing the country and handing his cases over to other officers. This is called a *turnover*. Thankfully, I had several months to prepare for the turnover of the case. I was excited about running a new operation, but the thought of taking over the management of this operation overwhelmed me for two reasons.

First, I was already carrying a full load in my CMO job and didn't have extra time in my schedule to read the file and get ready to assume the management of this complex, long-running case. In addition, we were operating in a difficult environment with significant counterintelligence challenges. Running a secure case requires the best tradecraft and total awareness of every aspect of our operations to prevent a catastrophic compromise by authorities.

My mind swirled with all I needed to do: read all operational reports that documented every meeting we'd had with the source; read all the intelligence he had provided; get up to speed on the counterintelligence demands of running sources in that particular area of operations; read cables and memorize the details of how operational meetings were carried out with him; and learn the dynamics of the issue he was reporting on, which was outside the scope of my counterterrorism mission.

I had so much to learn! There was more than ten years' worth of materials to read, dating back to the genesis of our relationship with him. Crushed by the enormity of what I was taking on, I told my manager, "I don't know how I'm going to do this. So much preparation is required, and I don't have sufficient time to dedicate to this case."

"I know," she replied. "There's a ton of information, and I know you don't have the time for this. How about you take one hour every day, just one hour, and dedicate it to learning your new case? By the time of the turnover, you should be ready."

So that's what I did. I took one small step at a time, beginning with the easy stuff. Every afternoon at a particular time, I dropped everything else and dedicated my brain to this one task. I didn't try to bite off more than I could chew. I pushed back on fear and intimidation by committing myself to a reasonable course of action. That's all I needed to do: plan my method of attack (start small and easy) and then decide the time each day I'd stop and switch my focus.

It's interesting how simple the plan was, yet it was elusive to me in the moment. My manager did me a huge favor by helping me see the project as doable and achievable. By giving myself clear marching orders and scheduling this activity into my daily routine, I was able to stick with the plan.

Starting is hard. Physical and emotional inertia are real.

The process of breaking through inertia applies to more than just large projects and big cases; it applies to everyday tasks as well. For example, when you haven't worked out in weeks, that first day back in the gym is hard. The idea of getting back in the saddle is so unpalatable. When I've gone a week or two and haven't been able to exercise, I trick myself into doing so by saying, "Just put on your workout clothes."

Once I do that, I say, "Well, I'm dressed. I might as well walk on the treadmill for a mile," or "I'll just walk around the block." Once I get on the treadmill or my feet hit the asphalt, I'm fine. I start moving and my energy quickly rebounds. Before I know it, I want to run. Thirty to forty minutes later, I've completed an intense workout and feel proud of myself.

Working out in a war zone was a similar challenge. Our leadership encouraged us to get away from the office and get to the gym. This was one of the few ways officers could let off steam: separate ourselves from work and preserve our mental health given the speed with which we were moving and the heaviness of the issues we dealt with (terrorism, torture, bombs, rockets, and sectarian cleansing).

But by the time we dragged ourselves to the fitness center each afternoon, we were already physically spent. After the first few days on the ground in Baghdad, however, I realized that I couldn't wait until I felt energetic to get up and work out. If I waited for this magical moment to arrive, I would never get to the gym. Counterintuitively, though, I could only continue my workday *if* I worked out. I had to exercise to generate the energy I needed to return to my desk and work until midnight. Of course, caffeine was helpful (all hail Mountain Dew!), but there was no substitute for exercise and the resulting good chemicals that surged through my body. The few days I was physically sick with a bad cold or cramps and unable to go to the gym, I struggled to make it to 9:00 p.m. Exercise was a critical part of my getting through that war-zone tour.

Waiting for perfect circumstances to align before you move forward with a project means that you will never start. When I'm writing a book, I don't wait for the inspiration to hit. I clear a space in my schedule, choosing the time of day when my brain works the best. I am a morning person, so this is my peak creative time. I have a window between the moment I wake up and two or three o'clock in the afternoon when my brain turns to mush. I don't wait for inspiration to hit. No matter how I feel, I sit down and start writing. The first couple of sentences or paragraphs are painful, but after I've broken the inertia, it flows.

I also don't get tripped up trying to write well-formed arguments and supporting text. That's not how the process works. When you're writing a book, the first draft is far from the perfected manuscript that lands in readers' hands. When you begin, you simply need to get the ideas out of your head and onto the page. And, as you move forward, the quality of your writing improves. After you've completed your first round and simply "thrown up on the page," you go back and edit the heck out of everything you've written dozens of times. Creative processes do not seek perfection at every stroke; they focus on getting the juices flowing and then improving the product over time. There is no other way to master your craft than to surrender to the imperfect start.

The bottom line is to remember that launching is the hardest part. That pain you feel at the outset will not linger through the project. It's the starting that hurts. You must be willing to endure short-term pain to break the impasse. Once you courageously take that first step, the energy it induces gets you into the groove. Sometimes something as simple as scheduling your next move takes it out of the category of "someday" in your brain and integrates it into your schedule so you can finally scale the mountain.

Confusion is the enemy. Anxiety is the adversary. Don't let them morph into scary mythological creatures in your mind. Flip them with action. Trample them with decisiveness. The idea isn't to do the *perfect thing*, just *something.*

What's the boulder in your brain that's keeping you from moving forward?

THE CONFIDENCE BARRIER

The things I feared doing when I entered CIA service—living in war zones and other dangerous places and dealing with dangerous people—uncovered unknown giftings. Because of my willingness to do those hard things, I unearthed the superstar within. I learned how to operate in difficult corners of the world. I became an expert on how to mitigate risk and survive extreme environments. I discovered I had a facility in reading body language and a high level of emotional intelligence, both of which enabled me to handle challenging sources. I mastered the ability to cull through loads of data to find actionable intelligence and unearth critical operational clues. I was no longer the desperate, inexperienced young lady who shuddered the first time I entered the lobby of CIA headquarters. I had slowly but surely come into my own.

Now, instead of being plagued with impostor syndrome, I found myself brimming with confidence and ready to take control of my future. Up until this point almost every career move was dictated by human resources based on field requirements. But then I discovered a fascinating position in the CIA that was way off the beaten path. No one in my direct orbit had ever considered this type of career move, so I wanted to find out whether a transfer to this particular branch was possible. I had a growing desire to spread my wings and felt the irrepressible urge to climb higher and push for more.

After a few weeks of gathering information about the job requirements and pitching myself to operational managers, I got the position. I was so excited and ready for a new challenge, yet this was a leap of faith. I didn't know whether the skills I had developed in the Arab world would prove transferable to working with sources from vastly different cultures. I would soon find out.

After obtaining additional training, I found myself taking on a case that centered on a part of the world far outside the bounds of my knowledge. The source was well respected and considered a high priority as he was reporting on a country that is a sworn enemy of the United States. Case handlers didn't have any counterintelligence or security concerns but wanted a fresh pair of eyes to review the case history.

While reading the case file and preparing for my meeting, I realized I was completely out of my depth. I became aware of how much I relied on my knowledge of Arab history and culture to guide my operational assessments in the Middle East. Without even blinking, I had known where the potential holes were in a story and how to confirm or deny what I was being told. Still, I decided to be positive; I wouldn't let the unknown hold me back.

After preparing for weeks, the time came for my face-to-face meeting with Miguel. I was warned ahead of time that his culture was misogynistic. I was used to that. But now I had two choices: either I could break his preconceived notions of my abilities at the beginning of the meeting as I'd done so many times when dealing with terrorist sources in the Middle East, or I could let Miguel maintain the assumption that I was an inexperienced or ignorant woman. If I let him underestimate me and he had been compromised in any manner, that could play in my favor: if his walls never came up, I might have a chance to discover whether he was hiding anything.

So off I went, strategy in hand. My meeting with Miguel was one of my longest operational meetings ever—nearly eight hours. I knew within the first few minutes of interacting with Miguel that he thought I was a simpleton. He wasn't difficult or aggressive, but I don't think he imagined my operational sophistication or level of intelligence. His assumptions about me were reflected in so many subtle ways: how he sat a bit slouched over . . . how he didn't seem nervous . . . how he answered my questions but never laughed or seemed interested in trying to make a connection with me.

Both his verbal and nonverbal behavior indicated that he didn't see me as particularly worrisome or worthy of a nervous kind of respect. He seemed to regard our meeting as merely a check-the-box kind of requirement. But I knew this response was unusual. Most sources were nervous to meet an officer from Washington, DC, because they were never certain why I was brought in to review the case and ask so many questions.

By the end of those grueling eight hours—in which I drove the conversation by asking tactical and strategic questions, processing his responses, assessing his body language, critiquing his answers, and mining for clues—I was wiped. I was so exhausted by the output of energy that I thought I was going to keel over. The cognitive demands of such a long meeting made my brain hurt. I had a massive headache. All I wanted to do was return to my hotel room and go to sleep.

And yet, despite the length of the meeting, I wasn't sure I had much to show for it. At first glance I hadn't formed a particularly compelling assessment of the source—either good or bad. And, boy, was that a blow to my ego. I wondered how I had been given such a great opportunity to help move the case forward and didn't have much to offer the handling officer and his leadership in terms of new insights.

Given my experience working tough cases earlier in my career, I understood the value of waiting before forming an assessment. There was too much data for my brain to process in the moment. I needed to take some time to consider all that had transpired. Rushing to judgment is rarely a good idea in intelligence, if you can help it. In this case there was no rush, so I took my time marinating in memories of the meeting.

After reflecting on the substance of that ridiculously long interaction with Miguel, I realized something quite interesting: it wasn't *what* he said but what he *didn't say* that bothered me.

No matter how many times I had asked this man why he was working with the CIA, I never felt as though I got a good answer. This man was risking not only his own life but also the lives and well-being of his wife, children, extended family members, and close friends to spy against the dictatorship that had a stranglehold over his country. His partnership with the CIA was a dangerous one. He was risking everything to tell us about the secret inner workings of a corrupt regime that trampled human rights. When you work against a regime like that, you are anxious to explain to another person why you are sacrificing everything for the cause. But nothing this man said was compelling regarding his motivations.

Although I gave him many opportunities to do so, Miguel never called into question the regime's miserable human rights record or the poverty its corruption had caused. In fact, I couldn't identify one single instance in which he said anything negative about his government. Why would you turn on your government and report to the CIA if you thought it was fine and dandy?

Bam! It hit me like a ton of bricks. Miguel was speaking like a person who represented the regime, not one who was working against it. This was such an essential red flag that it caused me to postulate whether this man could be a double agent. There were no other indications that would call his loyalty to the agency or his commitment to truth into question, so my theory wasn't received very well.

But I knew from my experiences in war zones that motivation is everything. There's nothing that drives me crazier than when I don't know what motivates a source. You can't do your job as an intelligence officer unless you have your finger on your source's pulse and know *what they do and why they do it.* Motivation is the beginning and the ending of the operational relationship. Despite knowing my assessment would not be well received and would likely be doubted and dismissed, I courageously penned my report and turned it in.

It took several years but eventually it became clear that I was right. My assessment was spot-on. The man was, in fact, a duplicitous double agent, working on behalf of a crooked government against the CIA. I certainly didn't want to be right about this assessment, but my confidence soared as I realized that my instincts were well honed from all the other hard cases I had worked.

It's so gratifying to be on the other side of doubt. The inner dialogue that used to plague each of my new endeavors, *I don't know whether I can do this*, had been replaced with *I can probably do this because I've taken on much harder challenges and survived.*

Don't worry if you lack confidence. Contrary to a common assumption, confidence is not the standard by which a person's capacity for success is measured. Your overall value in the world is determined not by how you feel but by your capacity to act. Don't delay until you have all the answers to your questions. Don't wait until you are "good enough" or have the perfect plan. Throw yourself into the depths of the imperfect and unknown, and eventually your progress will cause the shadows of insecurity to fade away.

CHAPTER TEN
THE PROBE

If at first you don't succeed . . . try, try again.

—William Edward Hickson, "Try Again"

The foundation of your get-off-the-X tradecraft is the probe. Inertia breakers get you started, and the probe keeps you engaged until you find your path. Probing, also known as penetration testing, involves systematically investigating all options to discover which one will work for you. In a world full of questions and possibilities, you simply cannot know what next step will be the *right* step until you try. And don't take any failed attempts as a sign you should give up. Every closed door gets you closer to the one that will open.

Think of yourself as an explorer like Jacques Cousteau, mining the depths for clues to your mission. As explorer-in-residence, ask a thousand questions. This is not the time to be shy or hold back. This methodology relies on the activation of the most intrepid parts of your personality. Agent 007 doesn't sheepishly move from one scene to the next. No, the person of mystery drives forward until they uncover the intelligence needed to get off the X.

LUCY'S STORY: THE HIGHWAY OF DEATH*

Thursday, August 2, 1990, began just like every other day as Joseph's sister, Lucy, got ready for work. She had moved to Kuwait earlier that year after marrying Michael, an Egyptian national who worked in Kuwait. After the wedding, Lucy joined him in Salmiya, Kuwait City, where he worked at the Ministry of Information, the central repository of news information and programming in the country, and she began work as a secretary for a senior Kuwait Airways official. The newlyweds didn't have their own apartment yet, so they lived with Michael's parents in a multistory apartment building.

That day, Michael's father turned on the radio as he did every morning. But instead of hearing normal music, the radio station—as well as every other radio station—was playing the same military song. That seemed weird. Next, he turned on the television. But instead of the normal morning programs, military-type music was playing there, too. At the bottom of the screen, an Iraqi flag and banner read *Marhaban bikum fi dowlat al-Iraq*, which translates to "Welcome to the nation of Iraq." The family thought it was strange but assumed the stations were picking up Iraq's programming because of Kuwait's proximity to its northern neighbor.

The family continued to get ready for work, and as Michael and Lucy drove along the corniche on their way to Lucy's office, they noticed a row of tanks buried in the sand with the turrets and barrels sticking out. They had never seen anything like that before. Then, just a bit farther down the road, they saw a military checkpoint blocking the road—also something they'd never seen in Kuwait before. Michael pulled up to the checkpoint with men

*Highway 80 between Kuwait and Iraq became known as the Highway of Death at the end of the Gulf War when coalition forces bombed the Iraqi Republican Guard units who were using the road to retreat from Kuwait after Saddam Hussein surrendered.

wearing military uniforms. A soldier asked them, "Where are you going?"

Michael responded, "We're going to work."

The soldier replied, "There's no work. Go home."

Confused, Michael said, "I'm sorry, what?"

One of the soldiers banged his hand on the side of the car and shouted, "We're telling you to go home!"

And then the soldier said something truly strange: "Kuwait is gone."

Michael and Lucy were seriously confused. The soldier's words made no sense. Suddenly nervous, they glanced at each other in concern.

Seeing that the car's occupants still did not understand the situation, the soldier announced, "We're from Iraq."

And that's the moment when the situation came into focus. Michael recalled a big meeting in Saudi Arabia the night before, a major diplomatic push to get Iraqi president Saddam Hussein to back down from his threats that he would invade Kuwait if his financial demands were not met. Was it possible that Saddam wasn't bluffing, that he wasn't grandstanding after all? If he were to actually carry out his threat, was it possible to march right in and take over a country before anyone really knew it had happened? Could an invasion of another country happen in mere hours?

Needing to figure out exactly what was going on, Michael turned the car around to head back to the apartment. He dropped Lucy off and decided to bring his father with him to his office at the Ministry of Information.

After Lucy arrived home, she received a call from Joseph, who at that time was in West Palm Beach, Florida, preparing to start college. He explained that Iraq had taken full control of Kuwait after rolling over the border in the wee hours of the morning. Lucy didn't know what to think, but she was able to get one more phone call through to their parents in Egypt to tell them she was all right before the phone lines went down permanently. It seemed the whole world knew what was happening in Kuwait before the residents themselves figured it out. Saddam had waltzed right in and, without any real resistance, annexed his neighbor.

When Michael arrived at the ministry, he quickly realized the gravity of the situation. As he approached the entrance to the parking lot, he and his father froze—cars were chaotically piled up. Drivers and their passengers had been shot by Iraqi forces, their bloodied corpses slumped over in their vehicles. The murders had happened overnight at the ministry, hours after Michael left his shift. The Ministry of Information was one of the first places that the Iraqis took control of after arriving in the capital city. Michael had literally dodged a bullet.

The reality began to sink in. The residents of Kuwait, most of whom were not Kuwaiti citizens, woke up to a city under the occupation of 140,000 Iraqi troops. The airport was shut down and international phone lines were disconnected. Within days, Iraq closed the borders of Iraq and Kuwait, turned back foreigners trying to leave, and warned publicly that nationals of countries that joined a coalition against Iraq would be sent as human shields to key Iraqi installations, including chemical-weapons factories, to deter attacks. Kuwait was literally cut off from the rest of the world. Everyone living in or visiting Kuwait was now trapped.

The invasion kicked off months of a forced lockdown during which only certain people, such as doctors and nurses, were allowed to leave their homes to keep hospitals and clinics functioning. Men were permitted to go out to retrieve food and other supplies, but for the foreseeable future, Lucy and her mother-in-law and visiting sister-in-law wouldn't leave the apartment, nor would most other residents of the country.

Day after day they waited, bored and anxious, for any kind of news from the outside. They had no idea what the rest of the world thought or how the international community was responding to their crisis. No news came, except for whispers through the grapevine about Iraq's torture and brutal executions of anyone they thought was a part of the resistance. The residents also heard about Iraqi troops' widespread looting of shops, government buildings, private homes, banks, and so on. The rape of Kuwait had begun.

Hungry Iraqi soldiers would go door to door seeking food or demanding clothes, jewelry, or other valuable items. Once, a soldier came to Lucy's apartment and asked for food. He admitted that many soldiers had no idea what was going on. They'd been told they were going to liberate Palestine and were shocked when they ended up in Kuwait. Another older man in his midsixties had been forced onto a bus as a conscripted soldier but didn't want to fight. He traded his weapon in exchange for civilian clothes so he could try to escape.

A few months into sitting on this very strange X, the situation devolved even further. A sense of lawlessness prevailed as supplies dwindled. Soldiers, more and more desperate, were now raping women and killing anyone who didn't give them what they wanted. Lucy didn't know much about the overall situation, but one thing she felt strongly: They couldn't wait for things to get worse. They needed to try to escape Kuwait. She'd heard rumors that maybe they could pay off soldiers at checkpoints to cross the southern border into Saudi Arabia.

After debating the wisdom of such a risky move for months, Lucy and her husband and several other Egyptian families decided to take their chances. Although terrified that it might not prove possible, they still felt they had to try. With a blackout of information and the lack of any discernible efforts by the international community to help them, they were on their own.

Four months after these families had been cut off from the world, a convoy of about thirty vehicles departed Kuwait City in the middle of the night headed for Saudi Arabia. They reached the border after only a few hours without being turned back at Iraqi checkpoints or military outposts or being harassed (or worse) by border sentries. It almost felt too easy.

Several cars got through the border, but trouble soon raised its ugly head. Saudi border guards started turning away Egyptians. Even though their countries were on the same side of this conflict, Saudi Arabia would no longer permit Egyptians entry into their country. Lucy's heart dropped. How could Saudi Arabia do such a thing? The desperate civilians were being forced back to their virtual Iraqi prison. The refugees explained that all they wanted to do was board a flight to Egypt, not stay in Saudi Arabia, but they were still refused entry. What would happen to them now?

Some in the group were scared by the border rejection, but Lucy and others made the bold decision to try another angle: they would attempt to cross the northern border instead, straight into Iraq, with the hope of being allowed to pass through the country. If they were permitted entry into Iraq, they planned to drive up through Basrah, northwest to the capital city of Baghdad, then west across the Syrian Desert to the Al-Karamah Border Crossing into Jordan.

This option was a desperate move. Lucy knew she would rather die trying to escape than simply sit on the X and die a slow death at the hands of Iraqi soldiers in Kuwait. She also didn't want to remain in Kuwait if and when war broke out. For Lucy, the choice was obvious.

Despite the knowledge of all the risks, approximately twenty-five members of the convoy turned around and started driving the opposite direction toward the Iraq border. Several hours later, they arrived at the checkpoint. With their hearts in their throats, they watched as one car after the other was permitted entry into southern Iraq. As Michael and Lucy's car approached the border guards and they handed over their passports, they held their breath. Incredibly, they were permitted access, too.

To this day, I don't understand how such a large convoy was permitted to leave Kuwait. The only thing authorities required of them was to head into Basrah and exchange their license plates for Iraq-issued tags. After a few days tackling that bureaucratic request, they drove north to the heart of Iraq: Baghdad, a place brimming with brutal intelligence agencies and their spies. These authorities were permitting their soldiers to rape and pillage Kuwait. Members of the convoy were rightly terrified of any interaction with Iraqis, not knowing what to expect.

If you've ever served in Iraq, you know how big a country it is to cross, requiring a minimum of fifteen hours of travel. Consider, too, how their progress was significantly slowed by the sheer volume of cars trying to make the great escape. This convoy couldn't hide. And it certainly wasn't fooling anyone. But somehow every car was permitted passage, and no one was harassed or mistreated. Kind Iraqi civilians even gave food and water to Lucy, recognizing her group as war refugees who needed assistance.

The last part of the drive between Baghdad and the country's western border, through Al-Anbar Governorate and the Syrian Desert, really tested their physical and emotional endurance. At multiple checkpoints they were forced to pacify the soldiers and pay bribes. Soldiers rifled through their belongings to take whatever they wanted.

When the convoy finally reached the Iraqi-Jordanian border crossing, they were tired, hungry, and completely exhausted. They had slept in their cars and hadn't showered or eaten a proper meal in days, and even their ability to use a restroom had been severely limited.

At this point they received the worst possible news from Jordanian border guards: "The border is closed for all nationalities."

Lucy almost passed out. How could this be happening? They'd risked so much to get this far, and now the whole effort was about to go up in flames.

What could they do? The border crossing was literally in the middle of nowhere with a desert in every direction—an empty quarter almost devoid of civilization. The closest outpost was about thirty-five miles away. Lucy fell into a heap on the ground and wept. She couldn't even consider getting back into the car, which had come to feel increasingly like a tomb.

As others, too, fell apart in exhaustion, fear, and disappointment, a kind Iraqi man approached. He suggested that they wait at the border in the hopes it might open back up in the next few days. He then led them to a nearby abandoned hotel and told them they could hang out there until he got word that the border would reopen. Days later, as provisions were dangerously low, they got word from the man at midnight that the border had just opened. "Hurry! Come now!" he said. They rushed to get back in line, then waited an agonizing twelve hours to get through. But they finally made it. Jordan allowed them entry.

Once on the other side of the border-control checkpoint, Jordanian security officials were not kind or sensitive to their plight. Instead, they yelled at the convoy through megaphones, telling them that the vehicles needed to stay close and drive quickly. They put soldiers in the front and back of the convoy to box them in. If anyone left the convoy or pulled over on the side of the road, they were warned that they'd be shot. For the next six hours, members of the convoy did their best to follow the lead Jordanian vehicles to the southern border of Aqaba for the ferry crossing into Egypt. But cars were pulling off the road because the drivers were delirious from lack of sleep, family members were ill, or cars ran out of gas. It was awful to realize, but people were simply dying along the way.

Eventually, the convoy made it to Aqaba, where they were permitted to board a ferry with their vehicles for the passage through the Red Sea to the Egyptian border. They waited much of the day for the ferry to push off from Jordan and then another eight hours after arriving at the Egyptian land border on the other side to be permitted passage into their own country. This felt like a journey that would never end.

It took several more days of waiting in line for gas to fill their vehicles and traverse the empty quarter of the Sinai Peninsula before arriving in Cairo. It took another half day to locate family members after learning that they had moved into a new apartment, but after the long and torturous journey, Lucy finally fell into the arms of her family. Lucy's parents, a six-hour drive away in Upper Egypt, wept to hear her voice over the phone, not having heard from her since the beginning of the invasion.

Sometimes a bold move doesn't work. In this case, Lucy tried bold move after bold move only to meet rejection after rejection under the most extreme circumstances. But because she wouldn't give up, or felt she couldn't afford to do so, she eventually pushed through to the other side. The Highway of Death and the seemingly interminable journey from Kuwait to Egypt had tested her mettle and resolve.

Sometimes you muster the courage for the bold move, but your gamble doesn't work. It's easy to get knocked off your game when that happens. We often feel foolish for even trying. But you must take a breath and figure out your next bold move or baby step. Like a good intelligence probe, test the network over and over again until you find a way through.

Lucy pointed out to me that the trauma of this experience has taken away her fear of obstacles. "Well, after what I've survived," she said, "I know I can get through anything." For Lucy, the Highway of Death, as scary as it was, turned out to be the very road that initiated their path to freedom. To reach your destination, you must look fear in the face and simply keep going.

INTEL FOR YOUR NEXT MOVE

Probes are helpful. They whittle down possible avenues of escape from the X. They show you which roads are closed and which options will not work for you. They help you realize not just where you *can't* go but also where you *don't want* to go. I have found that when a person is stuck on the X, some of the most beneficial insights involve figuring out what you aren't good at or don't enjoy. This intelligence decreases the options floating around in your head and helps you home in on your next move.

Think of the probe methodology as a powerful intelligence-collection operation. You are strategically putting yourself out there in the world to learn what activities move you and what makes the most out of your gifts and personality. Use the probe methodology to discern the activities that drain you of your energy versus those that set your pulse racing with excitement. This approach helps you identify your next steps by matching activities and opportunities with your essential self. You are searching not just for the open doors but for the open doors that match your specific strengths, as well.

But be aware: This is a process of trial and error. That means many options will not work. That is the point. There are a lot of nos on the way to yes. That's why you must develop a thick skin and approach this operation like a highly motivated intelligence operator who will continue probing until you find a way in. This methodology requires you to be intensely curious, tapping into your adventurous side. It requires a seed of courage and a dose of boldness. Give yourself permission to not be perfect at everything. (Imagine that!) Yet, while you cannot be good at *everything*, you will be amazing at the *right* things.

Some of us take longer than others to determine where we can plug in and shine. When you are exploring an opportunity and unsure whether this is where you ultimately need to be, bear in mind two things: (1) Are you growing and learning? (2) Does this thing give you energy, or does it gut you?

You might find yourself fascinated by a job, project, or opportunity before you have a chance to discover whether you're any good at it. But that fascination in the face of doubt provides the clue to keep going. I could not have known until I was in front of some of the world's most aggressive and violent human beings (terrorists) how gifted I was at dealing with them. It took me years of training and real-world experience to discover this. I had to be willing to wait for the breakthrough, for my expertise to build, for my light to shine. Despite not knowing whether I was any good, one thing I absolutely knew was how much I was learning. I was never stagnant. No way. I was sprouting; I was growing by leaps and bounds. I'm glad I didn't give up before I busted through.

How could I have known how skilled I was with HUMINT operations without putting myself out there and trying it? What a shocker that realization was. While we may be aware of our gifts, I've found that most of us don't know the myriad of ways we can deploy them. Don't reject opportunities or discard ideas if you haven't collected the intel and probed to find out what unique, never-considered path might actually be your perfect place of purpose.

Notice your energy—how you feel when you are engaged in various activities. This isn't a question about which is hard and which is easy for you. Many work projects are difficult, but they give me loads of energy. For instance, figuring out whether someone is a double agent is hard, hard, hard. But I love it. Cracking a tough case is fun. The calculus is not necessarily how easy a task is or how I feel in the moment but how I feel afterward when I consider engaging in that activity again. Do I feel a sense of anticipation or dread?

When I began building my public platform, I knew with all my heart that I was called to inspire people. I had always been gifted at public speaking and enjoyed it (thanks to my mother for putting me in dance classes as a kid). I also thought I would enjoy being a talking head on the news, a visiting expert to talk about terror attacks, counterterrorism operations, or foreign affairs developments in the Middle East.

It turns out I was partly right: I loved giving keynote presentations and hearing how I'd inspired my audiences. After these events I felt invigorated. Even though I was nervous and sometimes my hands would shake (especially in the beginning), public speaking filled me up. Doing live television, radio, podcasts, and social media events to talk about my first book and the themes in my book was incredible. I could do that all day, every day.

On the other hand, I found out how much I did *not* enjoy discussing breaking news on television or radio. The amount of energy required to prepare fact-filled sound bites drained me. I don't have a good memory for names and numbers, so needing to recall small details that could come up in a discussion with the anchor or host was not playing on my natural talents. I performed well enough, but it stressed me. When I was honest with myself, I dreaded having to do it again. That was a clue. Don't waste time on the things that drain you, but probe opportunities to find out not only which doors open but also which careers, projects, or positions make the most of what you bring to the table.

When my friend Michelle quit her full-time job to stay at home with her young daughter, she needed to identify a side hustle that would give her the flexibility to care for Hayley and work on her own terms.

Michelle's operational probes lasted for years as she worked her way through various business opportunities. Wedding photography was good for a season, but it wasn't a long-term fix because it disrupted family life.

Michelle then tried her hand at a multilevel marketing business for three years. It required a great deal of money to purchase inventory and a lot of her free time to get the business up and running.

But the 2008 market crash left her with a ton of inventory she couldn't sell. Plus, the extensive time and effort had not yielded much of a return. At that point she realized "the truth is in the profit" and walked away from that venture.

Michelle then waded into eBay. She went to yard sales and secondhand stores, found the diamonds in the rough, then resold those items on eBay. Over time, she found out what sold and what didn't, what made a profit and what didn't. Michelle worked her way up from zero to the highest ranking in eBay as a "Top Rated Plus" seller. This part-time business put money in her pocket that allowed her to care for Haley until her daughter started school.

Michelle is a master of probes and penetration testing. She used these tools to figure out what worked and to let go of what didn't. Both her failures and successes taught her how to run a business and how to market that business to the public, skills she used in subsequent career moves. As of the writing of this book, Michelle is thriving as a regional operations director for a nationwide dental and periodontist umbrella group.

All your probes don't have to be for big life developments. Consider employing this trial-and-error process even when you need to change up your eating habits or fitness routine.

Overall, don't be scared to try new things. My entire life is a demonstration of "not knowing until you try." I have broken all expectations of what I was able to do by pushing the envelope and throwing myself out there into the world. I would never have become an amazing intelligence officer if I hadn't challenged myself to embrace the unknown. There was no other way to learn this other than scaring the mess out of myself over and over again and trusting God with the results of those efforts.

You simply cannot know what you are called to do until you are willing to get so far off the X that you can't even see land anymore. Sometimes you can minimize risk by pivoting to explore options on a part-time basis (as Michelle did), and other times you have to leap off the ledge (as I did, taking a full-time job).

Your mission is to probe all the options in front of you until the key fits and you can walk through that door.

CHAPTER ELEVEN
POWER MOVES

Don't ever let someone tell you that you can't do something. When people can't do something themselves, they're going to tell you that you can't do it. You want something, go get it. Period.

—Chris Gardner, *The Pursuit of Happyness*

"Shoot for the stars!"

"You can do anything you put your mind to."

"Go big or go home."

These popular phrases encapsulate American cultural notions regarding opportunity and ambition: *the world is at your fingertips, and nothing can hold you back from achieving.*

But let's be honest: How often do we spend time dreaming, putting ourselves out there in uncomfortable ways, and choosing the next mountain to climb?

Perhaps, instead, we've come up with both real and imagined excuses about the obstacles in our way: unequal opportunities, uneven resource distribution, injustice, and so on. The reality is that obstacles will *always* exist. So do we make excuses and talk ourselves *out of* dreaming big, or do we talk ourselves *into* taking a leap of faith?

JULIE'S STORY: DON'T LISTEN TO THE NAYSAYERS

Julie wasn't feeling like herself. Nauseated for months, she was now home from school sick with something that felt like the flu. She doesn't remember how she came into possession of the testing kit, but what seared into her memory forever were the double lines staring back at her. Pregnant at sixteen? How could that be? As the realization hit her, the room spun and she slumped down in the corner of her bed in tears.

She had the whole world in front of her: she was a straight-A student at the top of her sophomore class, active in student organizations and cheerleading. Having a baby was what you did when you grew up; it's not what you did when you were halfway through high school.

When you live in a small town, juicy gossip travels faster than lightning. Before long, everyone and their brother and sister had heard about Julie Rigby and her shocking news. Julie was overwhelmed, not only by the circumstances, but also by the shame, embarrassment, ugly words, and sudden loss of friends who couldn't hang out lest they lose their precious high school mojo. It was a tsunami of bad feelings.

Even while doing homework and studying for AP exams, Julie grieved the loss of a "normal" life in the face of her new reality. And everyone seemed to have an unsolicited opinion on what this unwelcome development would mean for Julie's future.

"Your life is over now."

"You should give up the baby for adoption because you'll never be able to reach your potential as a teenage mother."

"You won't be able to follow your dreams now."

"How will you go to college if you have a baby?"

In the 1990s, teenage pregnancy was seen as the end of the road, rendering a young woman unable to reach her goals. Even today, having a baby so early in life isn't considered a methodology for quick career advancement. This life changer thrusts a young woman into an adult role before she has figured out who she is and what she wants out of life.

Nonetheless, the naysayers made Julie more determined than ever to prove them wrong. You see, my sister is composed of the same inner drive as I am, and there's no greater motivation than someone telling you that you can't do something. Such attitudes light a raging fire beneath us. You can be sure we will pull out all the stops to demonstrate how wrong you are.

Every decision in those early years revolved around the critical question of childcare for Julie's daughter (my niece), Danielle. So many wonderful people—in addition to our mom and grandmother—generously gave of their time to care for Danielle. This support network of family and friends made it possible for Julie to remain in school and finish well.

She graduated salutatorian of her class with a 4.0 grade point average and received a full-tuition scholarship to attend the University of Mobile (UM), where she majored in psychology. She realized that she had to make the most of the resources at her disposal, so the quicker she could graduate, the less of a financial burden it would be. So with a toddler in tow, Julie sped through UM. Not only did she graduate with another 4.0 GPA, but Julie completed her undergraduate studies in only two years.

She subconsciously continued to implement a strategy she has used throughout her life that I call *power moves*—the willingness to pursue a lofty goal or position that feels out of reach. It's the courage to take big leaps and despite how unattainable the option may seem, have the audacity to go for it anyway.

After obtaining her undergraduate degree, Julie applied to a combination master's-PhD program at Auburn University for a doctorate in experimental analysis of behavior. Julie finished her coursework, wrote a thesis, defended the thesis, and earned her PhD before I, the older sister, had obtained my master's degree. Julie's drive and determination were off the charts.

After six years in her first postgraduate job, Julie realized she needed a new challenge. She saw an interesting position at a company called Google, which she heard was a great place to work. Julie didn't know anyone who worked there, and moving across the country would necessitate an enormous life change, leaving family and friends behind. But she figured, *Why not shoot for the stars?* She executed a power move and applied.

Within three hours, Google's human resources department was calling her. Not long after, they offered her a job as a senior learning specialist. Julie reasoned that if she didn't like the job at Google or didn't enjoy living in California, she would at least be in Silicon Valley, a place brimming with opportunities. All that she would risk was an opportunity for growth. Rather than focus on fear of the unknown, she chose to think of *all that could go right.*

Julie thrived at Google over the next five years, in a variety of roles, before a job recruiter contacted her about an opportunity to work at Two Sigma, a data-driven hedge fund in New York City. In typical Julie style, instead of resting on her laurels at Google, she heeded the voice deep inside that kept telling her she needed a new challenge. This next power move took her from California to the bustling city that never sleeps. She made the great leap into a sector that she was wholly unfamiliar with, the world of financial products.

Once again, her growth mindset and adventurous spirit focused not on the potential pitfalls of this big move but on all the potential good things that could result from conquering a new field, living in a new city, and learning new things.

After three and a half years, another life-changing opportunity landed in Julie's lap: an executive level position at Chanel. (Yes, *the* Chanel.) Julie once again said yes to a position that she knew would stretch her. She transitioned from an organization with one thousand employees to the senior executive team of a multinational company with twenty thousand employees.

Gone are the days when Julie could barely put food on the table, afford rent, or buy new clothes. Her continued power move methodology produced a career, salary, and job perks that I've drooled over. (And it doesn't hurt that she has a wardrobe and handbag collection resembling a small boutique.) More importantly, Julie is one of the world's leading experts on hiring, developing, training, retaining, and getting the best out of a company's human resources.

Julie is a shining example of what it means to not allow circumstances to define you. The scared pregnant teenager whose future was in jeopardy made a decision not to let a surprise pregnancy define her value as a person. Neither would she let her new set of circumstances limit her potential or rob her of her giftings. Her early years were a hardscrabble existence, full of pain and sometimes doubt, but I am convinced that because Julie front-loaded the suffering, she has continually reaped the positive consequences of her sacrifices. Her indefatigable dedication to doing well in the small things and the willingness to sacrifice in the moment are what made the power moves possible.

Julie never felt fear about those risky decisions. "With each experience," she explained, "I understood that even if things went sideways, the net addition was worth it." Her world had already gone sideways at age sixteen. Once you face something of that magnitude, potential challenges fall into better context. For each of Julie's career decisions, she knew the risk was worth the gain.

Life is full of hurdles and curveballs, so you can either master the struggle now (get schooling, training, certifications, or knowledge) or struggle later when you don't have access to as many opportunities. Julie has wisely noted that "positive pain is productive," and I couldn't agree more. If you have the chance, front-load the positive pain. If you don't, remember that it's never too late to power move off the X. The only thing holding you back is you.

WHAT'S YOUR RISK TOLERANCE?

Julie and I are both good at executing power moves, although I do so with a great deal more trepidation than she. This is one of my weaknesses and something I must regularly work to mitigate. You may have a hang-up like I do with fear, uncertainty, or intimidation, but that doesn't have to define you either. To get past it, acknowledge what you're feeling. Then consciously push yourself off the X despite the thought obstacles your brain throws in front of you. In so doing, your tolerance for risk will increase.

Most of us have a healthy dose of fear and anxiety when we consider new challenges, but humans can learn to manage those reactions to move forward. When CIA recruiters visited Georgetown University to hold an information session and mine the university for new recruits, I sat nervously in the back of the library. I was in the final year of my two-year master's program and willing to consider any job I could get my hands on. The library that day exploded with energy, filled with excited students anxious to hear about a career in espionage.

But I was different; I was too embarrassed to even be seen there. Who was I to think I was CIA material? I was just a simple girl from rural Central Florida who couldn't get into the gifted program. I slinked in, hoping not to be noticed, and quietly moved to the back of the room. I was trying my best to keep a low profile. I was certain people would look at me and think, *What's someone like her doing here?*

But I was desperate to land a job at the conclusion of my program in contemporary Arab studies at the School of Foreign

Service. This desperation resulted in the placement of my resume in every job-opportunity box at the career center, including the big brown box labeled "CIA." Much to my surprise, the only call-back I received was from CIA recruiters a few weeks later. Apparently, they found my master's studies, international travel, and Arab-world experience intriguing.

A flood of questions ricocheted in my mind: *Is working for the CIA dangerous? What's it like to live undercover? What's it like to work in dangerous places overseas? What do CIA intelligence officers do every day? What does an actual intelligence officer look like? Who are these magical people?*

For secrecy reasons, the CIA doesn't tell you everything all at once. They slowly peel back the layers of the onion as you move through the process, telling you more about the career as they vet you and send you to the next level. The mountain of uncertainty regarding a career in the CIA was stacked as high as the Himalayas. I had a hard time conceptualizing any of it. Despite my natural inclination to be intimidated by new opportunities, I decided not to let it stop me from moving through the hiring process.

Forcing my brain to comply with the forward momentum of my chosen actions was a good thing. This is because working for the CIA requires high levels of risk tolerance, an ability to operate under difficult and often unclear circumstances. What you learn in the process is that every time you challenge yourself and take a calculated risk, you change. You develop new skill sets and discover unknown strengths. That hard-earned growth enables you to take on increasingly more difficult jobs or projects. Exposure increases tolerance, so if you want to grow, you need to remind yourself that this kind of pain is productive pain.

As you increase your risk tolerance, you realize that many of the things that cause you anxiety are activities that fill you up and bring you joy. I grew from being a homebody to being a person who seeks travel opportunities and longs for adventure. Embracing this newfound wanderlust enabled me to transition from being meek in temperament to brimming with confidence after living and working abroad. I was transformed from a tentative student of the Middle East to a person who is uniquely qualified to carry out difficult operations in challenging environments.

You don't want to be the person who drowns in an inch of water. You want to be the person who is experienced at jumping into the deep end because you have mastered the art of swimming against currents, moving out of riptides, and treading choppy waters. Taking calculated risks increases your tolerance for risk, yes, but this capacity-building process also builds your appetite for the next great adventure.

OVERCOMING ANALYSIS PARALYSIS

When you seek to implement a power move, you must accept the discomfort of not having answers to all your questions. I am regularly contacted by young people wanting to apply to a federal government agency. They often agonize over which agency to apply to. They want to debate the fine points of working for the CIA versus the FBI, the Defense Intelligence Agency, Homeland Security, and others.

I applaud their efforts to collect as much intelligence on the opportunities as possible; however, many of them lie awake at night worrying about which road to go down, and this indecision prevents them from applying for any of the jobs. They consider the bold move, but because they don't know which is the *ideal* course of action, they don't proceed with any of them. Perfection is the enemy of progress if it causes you to freeze.

I do my best to help them defeat analysis paralysis. At the end of the day, no one's offered you a job, so there's nothing to agonize over. Gather data about each opportunity, submit your resume, and see what happens. If out of the thousands or tens of thousands of resumes these agencies receive, one of them chooses to engage with you about a job, you can learn more about the opportunity and then agonize. But for now, why not just dream big and go for it?

For me, applying to the School of Foreign Service at Georgetown University was a power move. Applying to the CIA was a power move. Against all odds and thousands of other hopefuls, I got into both. The reason I stood out from other applicants is that I continued to demonstrate my dedication to learning about the Middle East. The surprising results of my power moves were actually the fruit of the cumulative steps I had taken to build a foundation from which the power moves could propel me.

While languishing in the in-betweens (where I repeatedly questioned my life's purpose), I made a series of decisions to advance my knowledge base. While applying to various jobs, probing career options, and peppering people with career-related questions, I didn't lie down and wait for my next move to magically reveal itself. I decided to pay attention to my interests. I was intrigued by the Middle East and felt compelled to learn as much about it as I could. Therefore, I decided to develop my skills. I bought an Arabic-language workbook and started teaching myself this fascinating language. After learning to read and write the alphabet, I enrolled at a local educational center to take Arabic classes one night a week. I didn't know where these small actions would take me, but that wasn't the idea. I was biding time while exploring what was next. The power moves worked because I had built a foundation from which they could spring.

Even though I am a person who loves to gather as much information as I can before making a big move, I didn't allow the myriad of unanswered questions stop me from pursuing a career that changed my life and is now enabling me to inspire others to get off the X. If I'd waited for all my questions to be answered and the path to be crystal clear, I never would have said yes to the opportunities offered to me. Without some crazy courage, I wouldn't have entered such a challenging field or traveled so far off the beaten path. If you're not a little scared by the opportunity, you're not trying hard enough.

CHAPTER TWELVE

CONTROLLED DETONATIONS

Nothing is impossible if one applies a certain amount of energy in the right direction.

—Nellie Bly, *Around the World in Seventy-Two Days*

Mindset is everything when you arrive at the base of an obstacle: Do you meet the obstacle with a surge of adrenaline or a surge of fear? Do you interpret obstacles as signs that you should turn back or as "business as usual" along the journey? Do you shrink back, apologize, or cower before an obstacle, or do you determine to find a way over, through, or around it?

It's important to recognize your natural reaction to obstacles if you are going to develop the muscle memory to get off the X. Early in my career, my natural inclination was to fall back, to retreat in fear. But you can learn, just as I did, to change how you perceive and respond to the challenges you will face when you're trying to press into your mission.

Some obstacles will not move no matter what you do. And that is your sign that there is another, better, path. Others will erode quickly and easily as you plot your way forward. The remainder are scalable but require strategy and planning. They might even necessitate a straightforward, aggressive approach, going right to the heart of the matter.

You cannot know which challenges are intractable, which ones are false, and which are temporary until you meet them head-on.

JOSEPH'S STORY: TERROR ON THE LINE

It was one of those eerily quiet mornings on the CIA compound, the kind that suggested something terrible had happened overnight. The compound wasn't bustling as it usually did every morning but was blanketed in a delicate, somber mood. Soon after I climbed the two flights of steps leading to our office space, I learned the awful news from my colleague: an Iraqi officer in the Iraqi Counter Terrorism Service (CTS) had been brutally murdered. A couple of days prior, she had left the safety of the government compound in Baghdad's Green Zone to secretly visit members of her family. She never made it back to base.

After not hearing from her for forty-eight hours, the counterterrorism community's worst fears were confirmed when her battered corpse was discovered that morning unceremoniously dumped in front of her family's compound. The officer had been stalked and killed by al-Qaeda in Iraq (AQI) during this fateful trip. They'd mercilessly pulled out her fingernails, burned her with cigarettes, beat her with fists, and drilled holes into her kneecaps and skull. The message sent to her colleagues was clear: we know who you are, we know your every movement, and if you leave the compound, we'll get you, too. If it was terror they were trying to spread, they certainly achieved their goal.

The threat from Sunni AQI cells was so tangible that the majority of the brave and dedicated officers of Iraq's CTS never left the Green Zone. They slept in their offices and went months, if not years, without spending meaningful time with their families. Their names were on a kill list, and the few who had tempted fate to attend funerals, birthdays, or other important family events had been abducted and savagely murdered by AQI.

The removal of Saddam's highly centralized dictatorship—which had kept a tenuous balance between Iraq's sectarian groups (Sunnis, Shia, Kurds, Christians, Yazidis, and other ethnic and religious sects)—had created a dangerous political and security vacuum. Without a hothead at the helm, plus poorly conceived Multi-National Force–Iraq (MNF-I)* political and security solutions, Iraq devolved into anarchy.

In AQI's bid to "protect" Sunni neighborhoods and villages from their enemies, their ranks swelled with angry foreign fighters from Tunisia, Saudi Arabia, Yemen, Syria, Egypt, Morocco, and dozens of other countries. As their numbers increased, we saw an uptick in ambushes, car bombs, targeted killings, and suicide bombings. In addition to their anti-Shia focus, AQI became more mafia-like in the way they targeted anyone—even other Sunnis—who didn't agree with or support their activities and objectives.

Sunni terror and insurgent groups and Shia death squads proliferated, resulting in the groups slaughtering each other as well as MNF-I forces. Both groups also targeted "apostate" Iraqis involved in the political process or security services. As if that weren't enough, internecine torture and assassinations hit a fever pitch. Groups on the same side of the sectarian divide then fought each other for supremacy and control. No one escaped the killing fields and collateral damage of the mayhem and murder.

After three years of escalating violence, support for the coalition to remain in Iraq was almost nonexistent. The US administration needed to find a way to cool things down, to create the political space for a noncatastrophic withdrawal from Iraq. Coalition commanders devised a Sunni engagement initiative to capitalize on the growing animosity between AQI and the Sunnis they were pretending to represent and protect. A surge of troops worked to

---

*MNF-I is commonly known as the coalition, led by the United States, the United Kingdom, Australia, Italy, Spain, and Poland.

connect with Sunnis to enable them to stave off AQI, strengthen their local support systems, and bring them into the political fold.

The Sunni engagement initiative sounded well and good, and we could see how the plan to engage tribal sheikhs could be effective against AQI, but there was still the matter of other Sunni terrorist and insurgent groups raging against Iraqi and coalition forces. *How in the world do you pacify or deal with those fighters?*

Against this backdrop, Joseph recruited an amazing but challenging source, a midlevel terrorist in a specific group that deemed coalition forces its mortal enemies. To give you a feel for the kind of guy Abu Hafs was, during one operational meeting he took a call from his four-year-old daughter, Amira. Abu Hafs put her on speakerphone so Joseph could hear the conversation and asked her playfully, "*Habibti* [my love], what do we do with Shia?"

In her angelic, high-pitched voice, she responded, "We kill them, Daddy."

"How do we kill them, *ayouni* [my eyes]?"

"We slaughter them with a knife, Daddy."

Joseph, of course, was dumbfounded and horrified. Observing this interaction between father and daughter made his blood freeze. It reminded him to use great caution in all his operations with Abu Hafs. This was not the kind of source you could turn your back on. He was no "reformed terrorist," but Joseph hoped Abu Hafs would continue to give us precious insights into the terrorist landscape.

In addition to the treasure trove of intelligence he produced, Abu Hafs had access to Abu Walid, a senior terrorist leader in his group. Given this connection, we hoped Abu Hafs could give the CIA the kind of information that makes intelligence officers drool: insights on persons and personalities that would be helpful in crafting an approach to tricky senior leadership targets.

When faced with a big, intimidating objective, you consider numerous ways to skin the cat. This initiative was the highest priority for the US government and the coalition, so our officers spent a great deal of time brainstorming creative ways to gain access to insurgent leaders at all levels of their organizations. We sat on the X, looking up at the giant boulder that cast an ominous shadow over us: the dreaded terrorist leaders who blocked our ability to bring stability in Iraq. The drive to engage senior Sunni terrorist leaders was an operational approach that seemed impossible, conceived more out of desperation than audaciousness. But, hey, this is what we were asked to do.

One day Joseph suggested to his ops managers, "Why don't I just call Abu Walid on the phone and invite him to a meeting?"

I remember thinking, *Call him on the phone? Seriously? You're going to pick up the phone and call a terrorist leader and say, "Hey, man, would you like to come over and have a little chat and shoot the breeze in the Green Zone with one of your greatest enemies?"*

What was Joseph thinking? That approach seemed way too simplistic to work, but it was, in fact, the most direct line. He would be targeting the individual who represented the biggest obstacle to rapprochement with the group.

Abu Walid was a seasoned Sunni insurgent in Iraq. The main aim of his terrorist organization was to reestablish the Islamic Caliphate in the country. In my mind, this does not scream *approachable* or *amenable to dialogue*. I seriously doubted that he would like to have tea, scones, and clotted cream with the CIA.

Joseph's direct approach was given the go-ahead. He was excited and nervous at the same time. If his attempt did not go well (and none of us thought it would), the agency would lose the chance to engage Abu Walid's group at such a strategic level.

With a master's degree in conflict analysis and resolution from George Mason University, Joseph was fully aware that the key to successful reconciliation is the use of a neutral third-party mediator. But here he was skipping that part completely, requesting direct negotiations with his foe. The chances of success were dismal, but Joseph figured that any opportunity, though remote, was still a chance.

Joseph knew he would need to deliver his pitch quickly, since Abu Walid was likely to abruptly hang up the phone. After a couple of unsuccessful calls, Abu Walid answered the phone. In his native Arabic language, Joseph engaged the terrorist, trying his best to sound respectful and nonthreatening. He introduced himself as "Sam," told Abu Walid that he represented "American intelligence," and said he was inviting Abu Walid to meet with him in Baghdad. A very shocked Abu Walid asked, "How did you get my number?"

The terrorist was caught off guard, his voice tentative, as he was clearly trying to wrap his head around the unexpected phone call. Joseph didn't answer the question but explained that he wanted to set up a cordial meeting to discuss ceasefire and reconciliation issues.

Abu Walid's mind must have been scrambling and sorting through all the possible implications of this call. We can use our imaginations to picture his thoughts: *Is the United States trying to lure me to be captured? Am I being set up for a kinetic-targeting strike? Were hell and brimstone about to rain down?* Regardless, he apparently realized the call made him vulnerable and could help identify his location, because he quickly hung up.

In addition to worries about being the target of a missile operation, he would have been terrified that someone would know this phone call had just occurred. If any of his colleagues learned that he'd had a conversation with a CIA officer (an infidel), they would consider it an act of apostasy worthy of a brutal death. Abu Walid himself had advocated such stark positions.

Joseph stood holding the phone in his hand thinking, *Well, that went pretty much how we thought it would.*

He tried calling the number every day or two, but it became clear that it was no longer a working number. Abu Walid probably had destroyed the phone immediately after the call. But that didn't deter CIA targeters who were hot on his trail. Before long, they had identified his new cell number and passed it to Joseph, who figured that he couldn't do any worse than he did the first time. Might as well try again! This was still the most direct approach to the obstacle in our path.

Joseph took a deep breath and prepared for the next attempt.

Given Abu Walid's fear of being targeted, Joseph was heartily surprised that after a couple of rings the terrorist answered the call from the unfamiliar number. "*Allo* [hello]?" he said tentatively.

Joseph calmly announced who he was and why he was calling, praying that Abu Walid wouldn't hang up again. Instead of slamming down the phone, Abu Walid listened carefully. He even repeated everything Joseph said and asked Joseph to confirm his phone number. Abu Walid said he would consider Joseph's proposal and contact him soon to possibly arrange a meeting in Baghdad. Abu Walid added that he might have conditions and would require guarantees of his safety and the safety of any other leadership he brought to the table. Joseph replied, "Absolutely. We will do our best to make you feel comfortable to come to this meeting."

Not long after this, coalition forces in Iraq captured Abu Walid at an undisclosed location. News of his capture traveled fast. Coalition forces cheered the detention of the terrorist leader.

During questioning, Abu Walid told his interrogators that the reason he crossed the border back into Iraq was to meet with "Sam." He then showed the interrogator a number on his phone that he had saved as Sam's. We don't know whether that story was true, if Abu Walid was really traveling to meet with Joseph, but it created an odd but amazing opportunity that Joseph pounced on right away. The next day Joseph was on a Black Hawk helicopter heading to the detention facility.

Joseph had to pinch himself. Here he was, a new case officer in Iraq, being sent to deal with one of the most strategic insurgent leaders in the country. Given his Arabic-language skills, cultural knowledge, and schooling in mediation and diplomacy, Joseph was well prepared yet shocked by the head-spinning turn of events. What had seemed an impossibility was now about to materialize in front of his eyes.

Abu Walid acted surprised and betrayed by his capture. He was upset, but Joseph quickly reminded him that he (Abu Walid) had not provided a heads-up regarding his travel or intentions, so there was no way for the CIA to have known he was coming. Whatever Abu Walid had been thinking, his only potential get-out-of-jail card was contingent on his positive engagement with Joseph.

Without the threat of being hung up on, Joseph could deliver his pitch in a more relaxed yet authoritative manner:

> Sir, you have spent a great deal of energy and resources fighting coalition forces. I'm not sure if you're aware, but we have no intention to remain in Iraq. We want to leave. But the more you fight us and the more you fight the political process, the more troops they've had to send to stabilize the situation. Meanwhile, you are being squeezed by AQI, which pretends to be your friend but whose ranks have swollen with foreign fighters. They are now dominating the scene—building their power base by stealing resources and destroying other Sunnis. Meanwhile, Iran is squeezing you from the other side. And you are worried about the coalition? You are spinning your wheels focused on the wrong things. We are not your enemy. The US government and coalition forces are not your existential threat. AQI and Iran are what you need to be concerned with. The more time you spend fighting us, the less time you have to focus on the real threats. So please consider laying down your weapons and stop fighting us. We would also like you to consider allowing your people to participate in the

> political process and populate local governing positions to save the future of Iraq's Sunnis.*

After some back-and-forth and light sparring, Abu Walid replied in a manner that surprised Joseph. He said, "*Iqtana't*," a forthright declaration that means, "I am now convinced." He couldn't have chosen stronger language with which to agree to Joseph's proposal. This phraseology essentially meant that Abu Walid was not on the fence. He was convinced that Joseph's explanations were based on solid justifications. He didn't believe that Joseph was there to trick him or yank his chain. Abu Walid was certain that what he was being asked to do, as a key terrorist leader in Iraq, was in the best interests of Iraq's Sunni population. At the end of the day, this was his main concern, so understanding Abu Walid's motivations was key to shaping the pitch that Joseph had presented to the insurgent leader.

Being surrounded by like-minded people in his terrorist bubble meant that no one had framed the situation in this manner. Joseph's distillation of the political realities was initially shocking to Abu Walid but now seemed glaringly obvious. Abu Walid was aware how much AQI was destroying any semblance of stability in Sunni areas and killing their own people. AQI's hunger for power and fight for dwindling resources had done little to advance the Sunnis' shared cause. What the terrorist groups were doing wasn't working, and Abu Walid needed a nudge to reframe his understanding of the precipice he was now standing on. He needed to reframe his thinking to get off the X, to keep Iraq's Sunnis from languishing in a place that kept their future in peril.

---

*While these were not his exact words, they are as close to the pitch as Joseph can recall.

Suddenly aware of the gravity of the situation, Abu Walid made one of the most important decisions of the entire war: He gave approval for members of his group to lay down their weapons and stop attacking coalition forces.

Abu Walid's directive had a domino effect as more and more Sunnis came to the same realization and decided they should try alternative means of achieving their objectives. Over the course of the next few months, attacks on coalition forces significantly decreased. Many Sunnis bravely, and at great risk to their lives, worked with coalition forces to pass intelligence on AQI, enabling successful operations against the terrorists. More and more villages were liberated from AQI's control.

What's fascinating is that Joseph did not employ political spin or tricky manipulations. What he did was simple, yet profound. While engaging Abu Walid by calling him directly on the phone could be considered a power move, it also demonstrates a methodology that doesn't dance around the problem. It hits it straight on the head. I call this methodology a *controlled detonation*. Sometimes we overcomplicate our responses to the obstacles in our paths. We do this because we assume that hitting the obstacle head-on will be completely ineffective. We think that complex issues require complex solutions, when it's often the opposite.

I learned from Joseph's approach that when you face a very specific and identifiable obstacle as you're working toward a goal, sometimes the most direct method is the one that will enable you to blast through the bedrock. By engaging a key leader of one of Iraq's most active terrorist groups, Joseph got in front of someone whose opinion and influence carried a great deal of weight. The impact of this engagement was far more strategic than trying a haphazard grassroots approach to fighters on the street, pleading individually with thousands of jihadis, begging them to stop attacking us.

In the risk-versus-gain calculation, what's the worst that could have happened? Joseph's call could have freaked out a terrorist leader, who would realize that the CIA had the capability to reach him or had some idea how to get to him—certainly not the worst thing that could run through the mind of a terrorist leader. Joseph's getting hung up on was not a terrible outcome. Fate, circumstances, or God's providence ensured that this direct opportunity was not lost but was carried to fruition.

Sometimes we make mountains out of molehills. But sometimes we really do face mountains. These are not invisible, self-imposed thought obstacles but real and often complex circumstances. When we run into these behemoths, our tendency is to awkwardly dance around them, seek to placate them, or stop in our tracks, transfixed by them. The important thing to remember is to not let intimation or uncertainty fool you into thinking the obstacle is immovable.

As in the biblical story about David refusing to be intimidated by the giant Goliath, who threatened the freedom of the Israelites, don't get wrapped up in the enormity of the obstacle standing in your way. When offered King Saul's sophisticated armor, David found this approach unnecessarily burdensome, as it limited his speed, flexibility, and dexterity. David cut to the chase, choosing instead the simple tool of a shepherd: the unpretentious slingshot. As a result of this bold decision, David's pebble hit Goliath squarely in the middle of his forehead, killing him instantly (See 1 Samuel 17).

This ancient victory reminds us even now to find the chinks in the armor of the obstacles we face and search for the most direct ways to blow those suckers up. With a little courage, a well-crafted and direct approach could be exactly what's needed to blast through the boulder blocking your way. Train your brain to view the obstacles not as scary adversaries or intractable situations, but as opportunities for miraculous breakthroughs.

JOSEPH'S STORY, PART 2: A TRIP TO THE VATICAN

What the US government and coalition forces achieved with the Sunni engagement initiative allowed coalition forces to pull out of Iraq. But those who spent any meaningful time in Iraq were aware that this process hadn't addressed the root causes of extremism and the terror ideology that had taken root. We reestablished a modicum of stability in Iraq, but we also unwittingly kicked the can of sectarian strife farther down the road. The inflamed divisions of identity and religion could not be swept under the carpet in a region that was a tinderbox for questions of power and control.

Conditions for the reemergence of the dedicated jihadis did appear only a few years later. Waves of popular discontent against corruption, unemployment, human rights violations, kleptocracy, and economic crises came to be known as the Arab Spring. After flaring in Tunisia, Libya and Egypt, the discontent of the Arab Spring sparked in Syria against President Bashar al-Assad.

Soon thereafter, the Syrian civil war drew in remnants of Iraq-based terrorists to reinforce Syrian jihadis who wanted to replace the Syrian regime with an Islamic Caliphate. Foreign fighters flocked to the region under the banner of the Islamic State (referred to here as the Islamic State in Iraq and Syria, or ISIS).

The fighters expanded their territorial objectives, turning their sights back to Iraq. In a major push for territory, they waltzed right in and took control of Iraq's second largest city, Mosul, in early June 2014. They soon turned their attention to Yazidi and Christian towns on the Nineveh Plains, which they rightly assumed would be easy prey. ISIS fighters surrounded these ancient cities and towns, demanding that their inhabitants convert to Islam or die. Frightened by the terrorist group's mass genocides, hundreds of thousands of desperate Iraqis flooded into Kurdistan, an area in northeastern Iraq under the control of the Kurdistan Regional Government.

The deeply traumatized Iraqis filled churches, mosques, sidewalks, and empty buildings all over Erbil. Temporary camps sprung up left and right, full of Iraqis who had no idea what would become of their lives as ISIS dug into their positions in northern Iraq. This inspired Hollywood producers Mark Burnett and Roma Downey to address this heartbreaking issue. They assembled a small group of professionals to find a safe haven for some of the persecuted Iraqi Christians who wished to leave Iraq. They brought together a fundraiser, a human rights advocate, and Joseph and me to figure out how.

Our part of the puzzle included identifying a group interested in obtaining asylum, then vetting them, finding a country willing to accept them, and managing the logistics of an airlift operation. This was a tall order. Where do you even start with an effort of this magnitude?

You start the same way no matter the size of your project. You kick it off by conceptualizing the operation, then brainstorming the necessary steps required for the journey (the ones you are immediately aware of).

The steps we envisioned taking were the following:

1. Identify a group.
2. Travel to that group, interview them, gather their identity-related documentation.
3. Vet their stories and basic biodata.
4. Aim for buy-in at the most senior level by delivering pitches to countries' presidents, prime ministers, or other high-level leaders.
5. Share vetting strategy with intelligence and security officials of each receiving country's leadership.

6. Work with receiving officials to determine their refugee-processing requirements, living arrangements, financial support, and so on.
7. Obtain visas for vetted refugees.
8. Plan logistics of flight operation.

Once you have the general operational concept laid out, you want to move your project forward as quickly as possible. We employed get-off-the-X tradecraft methodology number one, the inertia breaker. Joseph and I moved forward with the easiest tasks, the ones we could immediately implement ourselves. We began by choosing a group of internally displaced persons (IDPs) to work with, designing a personal-interview and information-vetting strategy and arranging travel to meet them. Small progress is significant progress for the energy it creates and the forward momentum it begets. Never underestimate the small steps.

Before we knew it, we were off and running.

From the genesis of the project, we all knew that the biggest obstacle we faced was finding a receiving country willing to take our group of IDPs. We were in the midst of 2015's great migration, in which millions of asylum seekers flooded into Europe from every conceivable direction. Every country had plenty of refugees, a flood of desperate humanity that severely taxed already-burdened social services. Asking the leadership of those countries whether they'd like to work with us to accept asylum requests was like asking a drowning person whether he'd like a little more water. It was the worst possible timing.

One of the obstacles we didn't anticipate was the need to obtain permission from the Vatican for their congregants to be part of this effort. This is because we had chosen to work with Father Douglas of Mar Elia Chaldean Catholic Church in Ankawa, Erbil, Kurdistan. Most of the displaced persons he was supporting in his parish were Chaldean Catholics. What we were trying to accomplish was against Vatican policy.

The Vatican's position was to maintain the presence of ancient Christian communities in the Middle East, the descendants of the first Christian converts. The Vatican didn't support efforts to remove members of the dwindling minority communities from the lands they'd inhabited for thousands of years.

Slovakia, the one country that appeared open to our project, stated that the prime minister and his immigration officials would not consider working with us without the Vatican's blessing. We appreciated this requirement because we understood the need to respect the religious authority of these communities. None of us wanted to empty the Middle East of Christianity. Even those who leave do so with their hearts broken, wondering whether they're doing the right thing.

But we also understood how disconnected this policy was from the current reality: Desperate families were willing to risk drowning in the Mediterranean if it meant they could get to the promised land in Europe. They faced death either way, so many families calculated that they might as well face death fighting for the chance at a new life abroad.

Recognizing this was the most immediate obstacle that was critical to moving the project forward, Joseph began planning a trip to Vatican City. Another member of the project's team, a dedicated Catholic, was concerned that we might be moving too quickly. She preferred to schedule meetings with Catholic officials in the United States first to build a consensus. She believed Joseph's idea was too bold, too direct, and, therefore, doomed to failure.

This was exactly the kind of bureaucratic red tape we were trying to avoid. Why start at the bottom when you can go right to the top, to the officials whose decisions drive worldwide policy? Why mess around with meetings and debates when you can go right to the Holy Father and his inner circle? We were trying to avoid complications, not add additional layers to the process.

This team member then expressed skepticism regarding Joseph's suitability for the task, since he was an evangelical Christian and not a Catholic. Joseph felt certain that his identity as a Christian from the Middle East was a particularly cogent point that would mean something significant to Vatican authorities. He was, of course, part of the population he would be discussing with the pope.

You will often run into people who, for whatever reason, want to complicate a task. Summon your courage and defy these pressures to fall into line just because "that's the way it's always been done." We're not here to do things that have already been done. We're here to do things of great consequence. We're here to break impasses. The army of doers requires people determined to take down obstacles, not erect them.

Against her better judgment, Joseph's colleague reluctantly agreed to support the trip to Italy. So off Joseph went to the Vatican in September 2015. Catholic officials in Slovakia were able to request the key meetings Joseph required, including a face-to-face with Archbishop Cyril Vasiľ, secretary of the Vatican's Congregation for the Eastern Churches. Incredibly, Archbishop Vasiľ was from Slovakia, and he mentioned that the pope's personal secretary was from Egypt. Neither of these associations hurt our cause.

After warm and friendly introductions, Joseph told Archbishop Vasiľ why he was there. He described his background, explained the project he was involved with, and laid out our request for the Vatican's support for our efforts. His plea was direct and to the point:

> Your Excellency, I am a Christian from the Middle East. I left Egypt at age nineteen to study in America when I was prevented from getting my education due to my faith. I understand how we need to be very careful not to empty the

> Middle East of its historic Christian population. My parents spent their lives supporting the Christian community, lifting it up, and helping it to grow. But for me, staying in Egypt was not an option. It was hard to leave, but God opened the door for me to go to the United States on a full-tuition scholarship to attend university. Years later I became an American citizen and had the great fortune to serve my new country as a counterterrorism officer. I have also spent a great deal of my life advocating for the human rights and well-being of Christians. I understand the Vatican policy to maintain the Christian identity of these ancient cities and towns, to keep Christians in their original homelands. But, also, who are we to sit in our ivory towers in Vatican City or the USA and tell other people that they should stay when we have gone?

What transpired next was the first big miracle of the project. Archbishop Vasil' smiled warmly and replied, "Well, Joseph, I think we are witnessing an ecclesiastical shift in the Vatican's position on this issue. What is it that you need? What can I do for you?"

Joseph respectfully requested a letter from the Vatican supporting our efforts to relocate some families from Kurdistan to Slovakia, or any other countries willing to accept them. A few weeks later, Joseph had that letter in hand, which he swiftly passed to Slovak officials. In addition, when the plane, loaded with 149 Iraqi Christians, arrived in Slovakia, Archbishop Vasil' made arrangements to greet the group planeside.

You can't witness a miracle if you don't boldly march into the unknown. The results of your controlled-detonation operations might surprise you, as the Vatican surprised us by blasting away any vestiges of a boulder in our path. Don't shrink back when you can meet those obstacles head-on.

PART 4: OPERATIONAL PLAN

So many out-of-the-way things had happened lately, that Alice had begun to think that very few things indeed were really impossible.

—Lewis Carroll, *Alice's Adventures in Wonderland*

Operational planning is the process used to analyze a mission and select the best course of action. Creative thinking helps planners understand the problem and design an approach to achieve an organization's objectives. Mission managers help operators determine when and how they might need to alter their operational approach in response to changing circumstances, obstacles, or other unforeseen developments.

CHAPTER THIRTEEN

GET READY, GET SET . . .

Good and evil both increase at compound interest. That is why the little decisions you and I make every day are of such infinite importance. The smallest good act today is the capture of a strategic point from which, a few months later, you may be able to go on to victories you never dreamed of.

—C. S. Lewis, *Mere Christianity*

The rush to prevent the next terror attack in the wake of September 11 drove government postings of intelligence officials all over the globe. Those postings took officers to chaotic and politically unstable locations and war zones where we didn't have the luxury to relax but had to remain vigilant, scanning for indications of hostile surveillance and counterintelligence efforts. The mission was purposeful, at times exhilarating, and downright exhausting.

Ten years working the counterterrorism mission finally took its toll. After tours to five countries and multiple short-term trips elsewhere, Joseph and I realized that we could not do this type of work forever. The inordinate amount of stress of a job in which you are never "off," the difficulty of being so far from loved ones, and the strain of moving to a new country every year or two had worn us down. We started to think that maybe we weren't meant to work for twenty-five years just to retire with a government pension. Maybe there was something more for us outside the CIA.

The proposition seemed crazy. What was life like outside the intelligence bubble? We had no idea. Were our weird set of operational skills even marketable outside the spy world? Would our counterintelligence and counterterrorism expertise be useful in real life?

We were sitting squarely on the X, depleted from the sacrifice required by such a demanding and all-consuming career. We had no useful resumes, few connections, and no public platform; fear of failure, intimidation, and uncertainty spilled out of our every pore. Leaving the CIA felt like jumping off a cliff. Trying to figure out what would come next felt like an impossible task.

Thankfully Joseph and I had a wealth of operational-planning experience to draw from. Maybe we could take what we had learned at the agency and apply it to our new lives.

As this big question mark loomed, we knew that we had no interest in going to work for a big Washington, DC, firm that was contracted back to the CIA. If we were *out*, then we were going to be *all the way out*. But to break the inertia, to get the ball rolling, we applied for a couple of contracting positions. We figured we'd explore what we might be worth in the marketplace and how we would be received by potential employers. It was the quickest and easiest move to make. It wasn't the perfect move, but it was *something*.

Applying for jobs that aren't necessarily your dream job is like viewing properties when you're considering buying a home. You can't know what will interest you unless you get out there and explore your world. Also, energy begets energy and movement begets further movement. Before long, a series of similar inertia breakers led to a breakthrough: we started our own company, contracting due-diligence and management services to a small firm working in Abu Dhabi, United Arab Emirates (UAE). This got us on our way.

For the next several years, a string of short-term projects paid the bills. Meanwhile, we employed a litany of power moves to market our services to well-known multinational companies doing work in the UAE and Saudi Arabia. We pitched our services to a broadcasting company to provide executive protection and event security for a major sports competition in Qatar. We submitted a proposal to work with a famous company that trains US law enforcement officers to improve their interrogation techniques. None of those big, strategic efforts worked.

We probed dozens of concepts to see which doors might open, which ideas might generate some forward momentum. We partnered with a US company to pitch the establishment of a canine training center in a Middle Eastern country to support its security requirements. We tried to get involved with government-to-government contracts involved in defense and intelligence training initiatives. None of the probes or power moves broke through the idea stage, so we didn't develop to a point where controlled detonations were required.

Our focus continually changed as some initiatives that seemed like excellent concepts refused to budge and others took hold.

Here we are, years later, running a successful boutique consulting firm that has landed significant international contracts. Most of our business is generated by word of mouth, in response to our rare combination of deep cultural knowledge, problem-solving skills, and diplomatic savvy required to do business in places such as the Arabian Gulf region. We're often called to help when business operations go sideways. We're asked to assist when relations between corporate entities and host governments are in crisis. We're brought in when surface knowledge is not enough, when deep operational experience is required to move initiatives forward.

Our greatest success has been in the following types of projects: risk assessments for oil and gas industries, the provision of security advisory services to companies traveling to or working in the

Middle East, due diligence and investigations for law firms and multinational corporations, and the mediation of corporate and legal settlements worth hundreds of millions of dollars for firms with a nexus to the Middle East.

Leaving government service was one of the bravest things we've ever done. (Besides entering service in the first place, of course!) It was incredibly risky to go it on our own. When I think about the scared, easily intimidated person I used to be, contrasted with who I am now, I'm astounded by the transformation. Getting off the X is really hard in the beginning, but when you master the concepts, you start craving change.

Being the protagonist of your own story is learning to dream big, think creatively, plan multiple approaches, execute those plans, assess the results, and then try again. In order to win you must develop the perseverance to get knocked down a hundred times and still be able to get back up again. It's pivoting to another strategy when your first or fifth idea doesn't work. Don't be swayed by the unknowns. Plan for Murphy to show up, create contingencies, and continue plotting until the door swings wide.

It's been more than a decade since we left the CIA. We have regularly employed the tradecraft we mastered to get off the X—using inertia breakers, power moves, probes, and controlled detonations to get past obstacles. We continually evaluate our progress and imagine what else we could do to move ourselves forward. If you are a learner and a grower, you'll never stop moving off the X.

Now let's talk about how that might look for *you*.

CHOOSE YOUR TOOLS

As your operations manager, I will be issuing you various tradecraft methodologies to use at will, depending on your circumstances and environment. It is up to you to decide which methodology to employ to determine your course. You may find yourself activating one or more of these approaches each time you feel stuck, whether in career-development decisions or everyday projects. The more you use this tradecraft, the more proficient you will be at getting off the X.

INERTIA BREAKERS

Inertia breakers are the easiest tools in your toolbox to employ, no matter what circumstance has landed you on the X or held you captive there. Since getting started is the hardest part, your best bet isn't to sprint or pole-vault off the X. Or agonize over identifying the *perfect* next step, as you might do in a game of chess. With inertia breakers, any small step will do.

Inertia breakers are designed to get the juices flowing. They lay the groundwork for probes, power moves, and controlled detonations of obstacles. They break the stalemate between your current situation and where you want to be. Don't worry if each tactical step you take doesn't result in an immediate change to your situation. Sometimes the first strike of the match doesn't light the fire, but the second or third attempt usually does. Any kind of movement, no matter the outcome, lifts the spirit. And since you want to conquer the landscape of limiting thoughts, this tool reminds you that *something* is better than *nothing*.

Don't be fooled by humble small steps. They can serve as some of the most empowering moves. Each inertia breaker contains the power to activate a dopamine hit in the brain, which motivates you to repeat the activity to experience the feel-good sensation again.[12]

What one small thing can you do today, even if your time is limited, that can start your crawl off the X? Consider coming up with five small tasks to accomplish in the next week that require minimal effort. You want to identify actions you can tick off a to-do list—giving you great satisfaction that you are working toward your goal. Inertia breakers generate the energy required to implement other methodologies.

THE PROBE

The next tool in your get-off-the-X arsenal is the probe. You will likely lean on this strategy as much as you do on inertia breakers. You don't deploy the probe when you are assured of the outcome—like a foreign cyberoperator exploiting a faulty firewall to break into a US government computer system. Instead, you use it to gather intelligence, to figure out what you are good at, what you enjoy, what works, what does not, what is possible, and what will never happen. Think of a probe as market research in real life.

For example, I recently realized that I was tired of my old fitness routine. Without motivation, I spent less time working out. So I used the probe methodology to explore new gyms and fitness routines to spice things up. I tried a high-intensity type of workout, yoga, and a barre class. I disliked all of them. As I was researching other types of fitness options in my area, I discovered a new boxing fitness club. In my twenties I took martial arts and kickboxing classes (both of which I loved), but I had never boxed. One trial class showed me just how much fun boxing is, and I signed right up. (Who knew?)

Don't discount activities, groups, or ideas you've never tried. If you're not naturally gutsy, this is your chance to employ your alter ego. Be bold and have fun.

Without obsessing over the outcome, what activity might you explore this week to probe your next step or gain a glimpse into your desired direction? Tap into the most adventurous and courageous parts of yourself and explore an idea or activity without concern for whether you will be good at it.

POWER MOVES

I define power moves as strategic steps toward something that seems like a long shot. Power moves are far from a sure thing. They are audacious ideas, unlikely paths, or dreamy options. When you picture yourself pursuing such a bold opportunity, instead of predicting failure and rejection, why not ask the following: "Why not this grand goal?" and "Why not me?"

None of the power moves I've employed throughout my life felt logical or attainable. Applying to an Ivy League school or to the CIA, launching a speaking career, or publishing a book—all felt completely ridiculous.

Yet here I am testifying that long shots are not only possible but ideal. In the process of pursuing each one, I discovered more dimensions of my personality and preferences than I was aware of. If I had limited myself to only what I thought I could handle, my life would look very different. I am so glad that even though I was heavy-laden with impostor syndrome, intimidation, and fear, I still mustered the motivation to grasp things that seemed outside my reach.

Power moves are not just moves you make when you feel stuck; they should become part of your overall life strategy, something you consider on an annual or semiannual basis. You may wish to ask yourself the following questions: *Where am I holding myself back? What big, bold move can I make that seems crazy and exciting all at the same time? What scares me to think about but saddens me if I consider not even trying?*

CONTROLLED DETONATIONS

A controlled detonation is a tool used against an identifiable and clearly defined obstacle in your path. When something stands between you and your little or lofty goal, instead of seeing it as intransigent, consider confrontation. True, some obstacles loom mightily over us. Perhaps some *are* immovable. Instead of interpreting obstacles as signs that you have pushed too hard, have gone the wrong direction, or should resign the effort, you may want to test them. Consider the possibility that you *can* find a way around, over, or through the obstacle and start brainstorming how you might do that.

As you put on your operational-planning hat to confront your obstacle, notice how that act of targeting it seems to change the obstacle's height and weight. When you stop fearing or avoiding it and start planning for how you will detonate, climb, or push past it, its strength starts to diminish.

What obstacle is standing between you and your next step? Once you've isolated it, identify the ways in which you might attack it directly. Like an intrepid 007, train yourself to demolish obstacles until or unless you've worked that angle over and over again.

There *are* times when an obstacle won't budge no matter what you do. But you won't know it's the wrong road or a dead end unless you do your best to extinguish all possibilities. If that mountain is indeed blocking your path and nothing you've tried successfully clears it, then employ the probe methodology to find another path. You can proceed with peace, never wondering whether you could have tried harder.

But watch out for imaginary obstacles. So many things that I believed were problems were just illusions of problems that never materialized as I pushed myself forward. Fear causes us to erect mountains that are merely excuses for not progressing.

Don't let real or imaginary obstacles get in the way of your life's mission. Use controlled detonations to attack strongholds. Kick off those shackles and get on with your next swashbuckling adventure!

TOOL BELT ON . . . NOW WHAT?

Now that you've considered which tradecraft methodologies might serve you best in getting off the X, where do you start? There is no specific order. You can employ these strategies one at a time, or pursue several concurrently. Just continually return to the drawing board to design the next operational approach until you have fulfilled your goal. Remember, this isn't a "one and done."

Getting off the X may take longer than you expect. I will share several important ways to augment your efforts and increase your stamina in moving toward your ultimate goal. In the next few chapters, consider some tried-and-true methods that have worked for me in the CIA, in my consulting work, and in life—valuable tools for getting unstuck.

CHAPTER FOURTEEN
MASTER THE FLIP

As for his slow verbal development, he came to believe that it allowed him to observe with wonder the everyday phenomena that others took for granted.

—Walter Isaacson, describing Albert Einstein's differences as the key to his success, in *Einstein: His Life and Universe*

Our ability to get off the X is contingent on gaining mastery over our mindset. We must learn to conceptualize obstacles differently in order to liberate ourselves from their grip. What's required is quite subversive: reframing our disadvantages into the very elements that can propel us forward. This counterintuitive reconsideration of our struggles flips our self-limiting narratives. Things that previously held us back become the mediums by which we flourish if we move forward with the determination to triumph.

TURN LIABILITIES INTO ADVANTAGES

When it comes to mastering the flip, examples serve us well. The following describes the kind of person I was when I started my journey:

> I was a girl from a small town who was ill equipped to deal with the world. I was severely lacking in knowledge and

> understanding of politics, culture, foreign affairs, and business. I was smart but not gifted intellectually, as defined by the school system. My parents and I had no political or business connections to give me a leg up. I wasn't aware of what opportunities existed in the marketplace world, and my parents lacked the worldly experience to guide me as I tried to identify my path and figure out my future career.

If I flipped this narrative on its head, here's what you get:

> I was so passionate to make my way in the world that I never gave up. Afflicted with impostor syndrome, I worked harder than most to keep up. I did everything I could to build my understanding of foreign cultures and international affairs by doing what others were not: serving on mission trips in faraway places, studying abroad in the Middle East, teaching myself Arabic, and working on my master's degree in Arab studies (pre–September 11). As a result of taking the less-traveled paths and building my knowledge brick by brick, I know my issues backward and forward, inside and out. My expertise is now off the charts.

Let's use this methodology again to conceptualize a job opportunity in the CIA. This partial job description is for one of the posts to which Joseph and I were assigned that we thought was the absolute worst place we could have landed:

> This war-zone tour is an unaccompanied one-year post (no dependents allowed). You will be expected to work long hours, six to seven days a week, and work most (if not all) holidays. You must be weapons qualified and pass a battery of physical exams. You will be more exhausted than you've ever been in your life trying to keep up with the flow of terror-related intelligence you collect. You will eat most of your meals at your desk and be tethered to the office, working with your colleagues at all hours of

> the day and night on late-breaking intelligence. You won't sleep much and will feel strung out most of the time. The temperature at this location exceeds 115 degrees in the summer. Expect daily rocket attacks. Numerous terrorist elements mill around the places you will live, and you must be careful not to become the target of their operations, as those never end well for the victims.

That job description doesn't sound particularly tempting to me. I don't think many people would rush to sign up for that kind of work opportunity. When we found out we were going to that location, I had a few good cries and many sleepless nights wondering what lay ahead. I was terrified and felt woefully unprepared to fill that position. But what if I flipped it? What if I rewrote the job description?

When I returned from that war-zone tour, I sent something of this nature to CIA managers to help recruit officers for the hard-to-fill job slots. This is how I described that same war-zone position:

> Limited opportunities exist to serve in a war-zone tour (thankfully). This is the best chance you will have to meet bad guys face-to-face, recruit them, and run operations against them. It will be the hardest tour of your life, but you will learn more here in one year than you will learn in multiple tours anywhere else. The depth of your knowledge of terrorism and counterintelligence matters will be unmatchable. Every hour of every day you will collect intelligence that will save lives, and you will hear about those triumphs from your military counterparts who action your intelligence. You will never feel more alive than you will in this war-zone tour, even as you are surrounded by death and difficulty. It will fundamentally change you and make you better and stronger than when you climbed out of the helicopter that brought you to the war zone.

Both job descriptions are accurate, but their differences illustrate how helpful it can be to flip the narrative, rewrite your situation, redefine an obstacle, or change your views of an opportunity. These two different descriptions reflect one of life's greatest contradictions: the harder something is, the more fulfilling and purposeful it can be if you approach the challenge believing that something good will come out of it.

At the beginning of the journey, you may find it difficult to conceptualize how challenges could ever work in your favor. I get it. I was there. But it's critical to note that simply opening your mind to this concept provides the space you need to move forward with grit and determination. In these situations, a little bit of faith and optimism goes a long way.

The confirmation that your willingness to do hard things is worth the struggle will take some time to materialize. This shift takes time because transformation takes time. If you don't give up on the idea that the flip is possible, you will reap the benefits of all the difficulty and suffering. At some point the reality of the flip will hit you like a light shining down from the heavens. You'll declare, "There you are! I knew all the struggle would be worth it eventually!"

You may feel as though you're pushing the boulder up the mountain right now, but just wait until you get to the top. What feels like an albatross around your neck might well propel you to greatness. Even if the project seems like a punishment or the job is beneath you, your commitment to the task and positive mental attitude enables the opposite of what your emotions try to dictate.

For example, in my case, what I thought was the worst option (an assignment in a war zone) cracked open a particular expertise (the ability to interact with difficult people and form quick assessments of their motivations and capabilities) that I couldn't have accessed any other way. In that particular war zone, few were able to process information, pinpoint questionable intelligence, or identify a double agent as fast as I could—that's the fruit of having read hundreds of intelligence reports a day and being up to my eyeballs in HUMINT and signals intelligence (SIGINT).

This triumph was the cumulative result of pulling my exhausted self out of bed every morning and dragging my tired brain into the office to read, process, and analyze more data than I care to remember. The job I didn't want quickly made me one of the most knowledgeable officers on terrorism in Baghdad and the Sunni governorates. The details that once drowned me became the foundation upon which I built my knowledge of terrorism in Iraq. The law of unintended consequences worked in my favor: the job I didn't want propelled me to a position of unmatchable expertise in my field.

The trajectory of my life and the position I now find myself in remain an excellent argument for the slow build. In my professional life I have never been a fast riser, but when I get to the top (after clawing my way there), I know my stuff inside and out, upside and down, backward and forward. By the time I arrive, there is no disputing what I know and how I know it. When I arrive, I'm not book smart, I'm street smart. I don't know things theoretically and am not speculating; I know them firsthand from the university of hard knocks. When you've served in the trenches, no one knows war better than you do.

What perceived disadvantages do you think you have that you can flip?

JOHN'S STORY: FINDING THE FIX

John Adams decided in high school that he wanted to be a pilot. His dream was to fly for a large passenger airline. At age sixteen he borrowed $6,700 from his grandmother to enroll in the Florida Institute of Technology in Melbourne, Florida. Their ground school taught the basics of flight, which included training in aircraft instruments and systems, engine basics, air traffic control, and more. In addition to completing ground school, students needed to log five hundred hours of flight time to qualify for the private pilot license, the first major step on the way to becoming a big-time airline pilot.

John successfully acquired his private pilot license, which facilitated his acceptance into the Delta Comair program at Jacksonville University, a private institution in Jacksonville, Florida, that functioned as a feeder for Delta Air Lines. He was so certain of his destination he rejected a football scholarship to pursue his aviation dream.

A year and a half into his studies, John was carrying out a training exercise called *instrument flight rules*, or IFR. In this scenario your vision is purposefully clouded to mimic situations in which your eyesight cannot be relied upon due to clouds, fog, and other poor meteorological conditions. The pilot trainees wear special goggles called *foggles*, an IFR view-limiting device. A certain number of hours must be flown using foggles to successfully complete the requirements for instrument flying.

With the training instructor at his side, John was flying the small passenger aircraft and carrying out a set of instructions that pilot trainees must repeat orally and then implement. Not long after beginning the exercise, the tower notified John of an incoming craft whose flight pattern and position were too close. The tower instructed him to execute an emergency turn to the left, which he quickly acknowledged and repeated before implementing the command. Unfortunately, John turned the wrong way; he went to the right, in the direction of the other aircraft, before the instructor took control of the plane, avoiding a catastrophic event.

To this day John doesn't know how close the other aircraft was. He knew only that he understood the command and repeated the proper instructions but turned the wrong way. Once safely back on the ground, John's instructor said something to the effect of

"John, I have noticed this with you a lot—the tendency to read the compass wrong or point the nose in the wrong direction. You repeat commands correctly but then execute improperly."

And that's when John realized that the learning disabilities he'd struggled with his entire life were affecting his ability to fly. When younger, John had such severe reading and writing challenges he was put into a special class. Most of the kids in the class had Down syndrome, but teachers simply didn't know what else to do with him; his issues were severe, but he didn't fit any of the existing categories. John was diagnosed with dyslexia and ADHD, but it was agreed that there was more going on. Doctors and educators never found an appropriate diagnosis for whatever cognitive or neurological condition rendered John's brain unable to process words and numbers. Learning for John was a slow, painful crawl, particularly reading and writing.

That day's IFR training changed everything. It's one thing to make a wrong turn in a tiny plane with an instructor nearby; it's another to make a mistake piloting a commercial aircraft with hundreds of passengers. John could never put that many lives on the line, knowing how dangerous it could be if he misread instructions or turned the wrong way.

Without warning, John's aviation dream had come to a screeching halt. He couldn't fly planes in good conscience even if he continued to work hard, defy expectations, and acquire the license. He could not risk other people's safety. And with that knowledge, John quit college. Everything he had set in motion to make his dream come true came to an abrupt stop.

If you've ever been in a situation like this, you know how it knocks the wind out of your lungs. John had nothing to show for all the hard work, all the years of study, the training hours, the flying time, and the tens of thousands of dollars spent on a career that could never materialize. John's severe learning disabilities had landed him squarely on the X.

What in the world would he do now? John didn't have a backup plan or a secondary goal. He had been single-minded in his pursuit of becoming a commercial airline pilot, but with the rug pulled out from under him . . .

At this point, many of us freeze.

Being stunned by an unforeseen turn of events is human. Grieving naturally follows. Yet you want to avoid remaining in that space too long. You need to feel the sting, acknowledge the pain, talk it out, process it, then push yourself to find the next step. If you remain in that grief for too long, what was once a normal, emotional reaction turns into a long-term posture.

Thankfully, John was not the kind of person to let present circumstances dictate his future. He knew he had to move on, so he went back to the drawing board and asked himself, *What am I supposed to do? What career am I supposed to have?*

John milled about for a year trying to figure out his next steps. One day someone told him about a state-funded vocational rehabilitation program for people with mental and physical disabilities. If you qualified, the state would pay for your entire vocational schooling. John was not above getting this kind of assistance. He'd take whatever he could qualify for. What was the worst that could happen?

He began the process to see whether he was the kind of student the program would fund. This required meeting with a doctor for two full days of testing at a special clinic. At the conclusion the doctor asked John what medications he was taking. John noted that he'd never taken any kind of medication. The doctor looked at him incredulously and said, "Given the severe learning disabilities you just displayed over the past two days, I don't know how you graduated from high school. I don't know how to categorize or label your issues. I've never seen a case like this before. Your cognitive processing is so compromised I don't know how you've managed to get through life."

Then he said only half jokingly, "You flew planes over my head with these issues?"

The doctor could not conceive that John had been able to graduate from high school, never mind acquire a private pilot's license. John knew his condition was extreme, and he knew that getting through life was hard, but he wasn't one to complain. He simply found ways to cope. All of the struggles he had endured had developed in him a dogged determination to push forward.

John qualified for the full-tuition vocational program. Now he just had to figure out what to do. He entertained various options, such as aircraft mechanic, real estate entrepreneur, and electrician.

One day, after he gave a friend a shoulder massage, she noted, "You are really good at this. You should consider becoming a massage therapist."

John had never considered such a thing before. He thought it was a "woman's job." But the comment planted a seed that, over the course of several months, started to grow. Intrigued by the idea of learning about the human body, John visited the Florida College of Natural Health and toured its massage therapy program.

He loved what he saw. Anatomy and the mechanics of movement fascinated him the way that plane design and aerodynamics did. He could not wait to dive into this new course of study.

Despite severe learning disabilities and a dislike of school, John realized how much he loved learning. And when you love something, you'll do anything to adapt and process what you need to learn.

John eventually acquired an associate's degree in science and natural health and kicked off his unexpected career as a massage therapist. But that's not the end of the story.

He soon realized he didn't enjoy giving the typical feel-good, Swedish-type massages. What really challenged him were patients with movement problems that no one else seemed able to alleviate or fix. These people had seen multiple doctors and physical therapists but languished in pain or experienced severely limited range of motion.

John knew what it was like to explore, identify, and exploit alternative avenues to forge successful new paths. So he used this same approach to develop ways to treat the body's mechanical problems. John's sense of touch and keen sense of the mechanics of motion were critical to diagnose the problems and develop therapeutic approaches for each client. His broken brain circuitry in some areas has led to massive giftings in others. John's coping mechanisms have rendered him an outstanding student of the human body and an empathetic and committed therapist who can solve problems for patients who can't get help anywhere else.

When I met John twenty years into his career, his business, Fix Therapy, was thriving as one of the most cutting-edge massage therapy clinics in the country. He was so popular that it was hard to get an appointment.

John loves what he does. For him, this career is not a job; it's a calling. He couldn't be happier (and neither could his patients). Despite John's rocky start, he ended up in the perfect place. His unexpected career has had an undeniable impact on so many people, in a way that being a pilot could not.

John soon realized he had the knowledge needed to flip an industry ripe for change. Why do it the way it's always been done when there's a better way?

He is now training other therapists in his methodology and giving them the business plan and marketing tools to challenge a largely stagnant industry poised for transformation.

That's exactly what I'd expect from John. His dedication to learning and growing means that he doesn't freeze when told what he can't do. He stubbornly moves off the X to focus on what he *can* control. He flips his disadvantages and allows time, focus, and perseverance to turn them into his greatest advantage.

Out of pain comes promise if you don't let yourself be defined by what may have seemed like limitations.

May we all have that kind of forward momentum, where we acknowledge and feel the pain but move forward anyway. If you recall basic mathematics, X represents the unknown. The value of X has to be worked out in mathematical equations. So, too, is the effort to discover what's next. Instead of thinking of this mystery as a burden, think of it as a great adventure. If you approach the unknown this way, the heft of the search is greatly relieved. The pursuit of your next step feels more doable.

CHAPTER FIFTEEN

LAUNCH AN X OPERATIONS GROUP

The best way to have a good idea is to have lots of ideas.

—Linus Pauling, winner of the 1954 Nobel Prize in Chemistry and the 1962 Nobel Peace Prize

Beginning in training and continuing through our CIA careers, operational managers regularly sat down with their teams to brainstorm ways to meet operational objectives. We would discuss a potential target and then think of various ways to get at the target. The creative approaches that emerged from these ops groups were critical in helping us find ways to connect with hard targets or move other challenging operational initiatives forward.

Basically, we used the power of the group to get off the X.

We included officers at various stages of their careers and people who'd served in a variety of locations. This diversity of experience and opinions helped expand our conception of what could be done and how we could do it. Whenever someone said, "One time this particular approach worked for me," they would offer an idea that we'd never considered but inevitably ended up being the approach that led to the breakthrough we desperately needed. Or if someone warned, "I'd stay away from that because a, b, and c," we could avoid pitfalls or methods that didn't work. Two minds are better than one, and several minds can be the catalyst for a powerful explosion of ideas.

When the CIA came the closest it ever had to identifying the location of al-Qaeda founder Osama bin Laden, it was maddening to know he might slip through our fingers because we could not confirm his identity. We were unable to figure out whether the shadow of the tall guy in the compound in Abbottabad, Pakistan—whose face and body couldn't be seen from any angle—was the most wanted terrorist in US history. This individual became known as the Pacer due to his daily walks back and forth across the compound. He was safely ensconced in his strange villa, and no amount of effort seemed to coax him or anyone else out of the compound. If the president of the United States was to authorize US Special Forces to penetrate deep into another country's sovereign territory, he had to be as sure as possible that the target was indeed bin Laden.

CIA director Leon Panetta eventually hit a boiling point of frustration because the team working on this thorny top-secret problem didn't have any new ideas. He demanded that the exhausted, overworked, burdened crew of intelligence analysts and operators come up with ten new ideas to determine whether the Pacer was bin Laden. Jeremy Bash, the CIA's chief of staff, upped the ante and encouraged them to come up with twenty-five.

"Suggest anything, no matter how outlandish," he said. "Don't worry about whether you can do it. Don't worry about whether it's a good idea. Just put it on a piece of paper." He was looking to reinvigorate the tired bunch.

The group surprised their superiors and came up with thirty-eight. Some were outrageous, others crazy and unrealistic, but a few could help produce helpful intelligence. Panetta didn't know whether any of it would lead to new information but later noted that "wild ideas were better than no ideas at all."

At the end of the exercise, "Panetta could feel energy surging back into the group. . . . That's what he wanted more than anything else. That, and Osama bin Laden—dead or alive."[13]

When you form an ops group like this and begin discussing plans and dreams with like-minded individuals, you spark motivation and build confidence for the next steps. This brainstorming gets the blood flowing and puts a spring in your step as you open yourself to the creative possibilities. Like an intelligence officer, you can raise the what-ifs and why-nots. You can learn ways to manage risk and move yourself forward efficiently when others share their hard-won wisdom with you (and you share yours).

During our first tour, Joseph and I considered various strategies to get to a hard target we had met at an event. This person (we'll call him Ridwan) tried to avoid contact with Americans, as our countries were not friends. Yet Ridwan appeared to be a kind man and seemed fascinated by us. We got the feeling that we would have been good friends if our countries were not locked in a diplomatic standoff.

But no matter how hard we tried, we couldn't secure a meeting with this gentleman. He was too scared to meet or interact with us. That's why Joseph and I felt we should do our best to get in front of Ridwan. We wanted him to see us as open, accessible, and trustworthy should he ever want to switch sides. If the political landscape in his country changed and he suddenly felt the need to collaborate with the United States, he would know whom to engage.

One day while we were brainstorming, we asked our colleagues for ideas on how to engineer face-to-face interactions with our hard target. Everyone threw out ideas left and right. After about five minutes, our boss came up with what seemed like a winning idea with minimal risk to both parties. He asked, "Michele, you like to bake cakes, right?"

"Yes, I love to bake."

"Why don't you bake him a cake for his birthday next week. And then show up at his residence and give it to him. Don't call. Don't ask. Just show up at the gate."

As soon as he said it, Joseph and I responded, "Yes! That's it—that's a brilliant idea."

We were banking on the assumption that no one can turn down such a thoughtful gesture, especially when it's homemade. And wouldn't you know it? My triple-layer chocolate cake did the trick. It literally got us in the door and provided the opening we needed to connect with our hard target when nothing else would work.

The free-flowing ideas generated in an ops group help participants creatively map their ways off the X. You can often find an immediate solution because someone else has been there and done that. They've already conquered that challenge, so why recreate the wheel of hardship?

Be sure to tap into your group for more than brainstorming, though. One year, after interviewing a highly valued source in a sensitive country, I realized I couldn't quite discern the nonverbal behavior I'd observed. So I swallowed my pride and said to my manager, "I need help."

A group of seasoned officers stopped what they were doing, gathered around, and started asking me questions. They teased all kinds of information out of me: What was I feeling? Why did I feel that way? What questions seemed problematic or were left unanswered in the meeting? What nonverbals did I observe?

All the experience they had accumulated in their own careers was brought to bear in eliciting details from me, brainstorming insights, and pointing me to a potential breakthrough. My colleagues' critical counterintelligence questions would guide the next steps with the case.

Both examples showcase how an X ops group amplifies the resources and experience available to you and helps you get unstuck. Chances are, someone in your circle knows an easier way, a better avenue, or a creative approach. Or they can encourage you to tap into your own intuition.

Basically, think of these gatherings as safe spaces you create, as needed, to collect intelligence, plan your operations, and plot your next move. Who might you invite into *your* X ops group?

CREATE A PROOF OF CONCEPT

After you come up with ideas in your ops group, you want to prove your concept by trying out various options. But don't bite off more than you can chew. Sometimes when we're plotting to get off the X and have big dreams, we overdo it. For example, we think we need to plan for our brand-new Amazon store to sell every object, all over the world, to everyone, all the time. We often end up overwhelmed, confused, and defeated by our unachievable objectives.

Instead, we need to begin with a proof of concept, such as the building of an online store for the purchase of books. Start small, test our theories, see whether an idea gains traction, and then expand. Beginning with bite-size projects prevents us from overwhelming ourselves with an outcome we can't possibly reach at that moment.

This operational approach is similar to the "spaghetti" concept: throw the spaghetti at the wall and see what sticks. Developing a more measured ground plan is a risk-mitigation tool. It forces us to take more doable steps to get off the X, maximizing our success with inertia breakers and probes, which can eventually lay the groundwork for expansion.

Proof of concept works differently, however, when you're dealing with circumstances beyond your control—when you're pushed into new territory you never anticipated, clubs you'd never want to join. I'm thinking of head spinners such as an unexpected job loss, a health crisis, legal woes, divorce, or the death of a loved one.

Attempting to identify some kind of long-term motivation doesn't apply when you're trying to survive the next minute or the next hour. In these instances, proof of concept involves finding an activity that can pull you out of the pain, even if only as a temporary reprieve. It means searching for something that brings a little bit of light in an otherwise dark space.

When you find and engage in such an activity, the proof of concept is a glimmer of hope that a day will come when the distance between pain and joy is farther apart. Over time these activities can move you off the X of shock and grief and move you toward healing.

When I've found myself in the middle of a storm, I've worked hard to identify a proof of concept to survive. I've discovered easy things I can do to bring temporary relief. What's fascinating, though, is that I've unwittingly planted seeds that might expand into larger initiatives.

When reeling from the death of a family member and dealing with relationship pain, I wrote. Eventually, those musings turned into an inspirational memoir that's touched tens of thousands of lives. When I was experiencing deep persecution that threatened all I had ever worked for, I climbed out of the muck by focusing on the needs of others. The efforts to get my eyes off the excruciating pain morphed into providing support to nonprofits working in my city.

Proof of concept is a hook you can grab onto, activities successful in small measure that you can replicate or expand upon.

Now that you understand the secret of the flip and the power of an X ops group, what idea or dream do you want to start brainstorming with like-minded friends or family?

CHAPTER SIXTEEN
TRAIN THE BRAIN

What you focus on, that's where you'll drive.

—CIA high-performance driving instructors

During the paramilitary portion of our operational training, we spent a week doing high-performance driving exercises. The CIA's driving instructors were trying to get us to think differently about our vehicles and what they could do for us, particularly if we were ambushed by an enemy or threatened while in our vehicles. Instructors began the training by telling us that, on average, a driver uses only a small percentage of a car's power and capacity. One of the course objectives was to push students to explore the vehicles' capabilities and expand our understanding of their limits. The clear message was that a car could take quite a beating, still perform well, and protect its occupants. They wanted us to develop confidence in our driving machines. And to drive the point home, we weren't driving Aston Martins or McLarens; we were driving banged-up old cars that had been abused by the students, class after class.

As with most challenges, the biggest obstacle was the battleground of our minds. Gaining mastery over our fear and hesitancy was a critical first lesson. As we drove laps around a large rectangular course with curved corners, an instructor sat beside each of us in the passenger seat. We were told to accelerate on the straightaways. That wasn't the hard part. The difficulty came in holding that speed until the very last moment as instructors taught us the art of controlled braking and the techniques for navigating curves and corners to maximize speed and maintain full control.

I'm the type of driver who appreciates torque and acceleration, but seeing the corner coming at me so quickly and being told "Hold your speed. Don't touch that brake. Maintain your speed" was hard. As I raced toward the trees at the end of the track, my brain screamed, *Brake! Brake!* Right before it looked as if I might fly off the track and into the woods, my instructor finally said, "Okay, squeeze the brakes." I heeded his instructions for a controlled deceleration as I drove into the curve and then through it. Never were we instructed to slam on the brakes. Instead, we were repeatedly reminded to *press* them, because "smooth is fast."

Trusting the instructor and his years of driving experience showed me I could deliver far more than I thought. He knew the limits of the vehicle better than I, so it behooved me to heed every bit of instruction. With each lap around the circuit in which I didn't crash and burn, my confidence increased. The track became more and more fun with my growing mastery and control. Having an expert in your sphere to calm your nerves and help you manage the twists and turns of life mitigates the stress of the unknowns.

The second major learning point was to look ahead. Student drivers had to be reminded to keep their eyes on the course, not on the speedometer or the tree line behind the curve. Instructors were trying to instill the discipline of looking past the curve we were navigating. They kept reminding their charges, "What you focus on, that's where you'll drive." They were trying to get us to look ahead, to keep our eyes on where we wanted to go. One of my colleagues lost that focus and drove into a tree. Thankfully he wasn't hurt, but it was a real-life reminder not to fall in love with the foliage.

Another important lesson involved responding appropriately to unexpected obstacles. Once again, the exercises were designed to widen our field of vision, so the obstacles didn't dominate our attention. The instructors wanted us to identify alternatives by looking at the bigger picture.

While we were stationary, the instructor would put a large piece of cardboard in front of each student driver, blocking our vision. We were then asked to shift the car into drive and accelerate to between thirty-five and forty miles per hour. The instructor held the top of the steering wheel with his left hand to keep the car moving forward in a straight line while the student maintained the proper speed. Our hands held lightly to the wheel, waiting for the moment when the instructor pulled away the cardboard, let go of the steering wheel, and gave us full control of the vehicle. We were told to react to whatever we saw by veering to the right or to the left.

We were immediately confronted with large foam boxes that blocked our path. Some students couldn't respond quickly enough and busted through the obstacles set out in formation in front of us. The foam blocks flew in every direction. I'm pretty sure that the same guy who ran into the tree also hit the foam walls his instructors had erected. But those who kept a wider field of vision and maintained a good focus on what was ahead were able to pull to the left or right when presented with a fake wall or an obstruction in the road. They kept their focus wide so that when the cardboard was snatched away and they were presented with a difficult situation, they had the right reaction.

Mental fitness and emotional acuity are hard to maintain. Especially when you're exhausted or overwhelmed by an obstacle or see no end to the in-between—the periods of time when it feels like nothing is working. But you must force yourself. Yell a little. Let 'er rip on the punching bag. Eat a pint of ice cream. Endure the occasional meltdown. Then afterward get back up again, dust yourself off, and raise those eyes.

When you are trying to survive the awful in-betweens, what you put into your brain matters. Limit your social media, which tends to feed anxiety or induce malaise. Train your brain to focus on people and activities that will lift you up. Proactively fill your mind with positivity to counteract the very human inclination to doubt your chances for success. And finally, the most important way to pull yourself out of the vacuousness of being lost, frustrated, and confused, is to redeem that vapidity by doing something for someone else. Give. Love. Serve. Every step outside yourself counteracts the chaos within.

Are you focusing on something right now that's feeding anxiety instead of fighting it? Are you isolating and spending more time on social media than plotting your next move? Remember: What you focus on, that's where you'll drive.

GLENN'S STORY: LAYOVERS IN HELL

As I mentioned in Lucy's Story in Chapter 10, the entire world was shocked when Iraq invaded its neighbor, the tiny nation-state of Kuwait, on August 2, 1990. Most didn't see it coming, even though Saddam Hussein had threatened the move repeatedly and had amassed a significant number of troops on the Iraq-Kuwait border. Everyone thought Saddam was saber-rattling, but, alas, he actually meant what he said. His new war was an act of desperation but one that had far-reaching effects.

Kuwait had been demanding repayment of its $14 billion loan to Iraq, which had funded Saddam's ten-year war with Iran.

Simultaneously, Kuwait was unwilling to decrease its oil production, which kept driving down the price of petroleum products and adding to Iraq's financial woes.

In addition to the mounting debts, Saddam started manufacturing a narrative of economic injustice: he accused Kuwait of stealing oil from the Rumaila oil field, which ran beneath both countries, bringing additional financial harm to Iraq. Saddam used this allegation in an attempt to drum up support and justify threatening Kuwait over the purported injustice. Worried what he might do next, officials from Egypt and Saudi Arabia met with all the parties to mediate the political crisis and fend off a military incursion.

Meanwhile, the world community went about its business, secure in the assumption that the diplomatic efforts would calm the storm. But as we all know, these assumptions turned out to be incorrect.

Saddam's flash invasion took everyone by surprise. This included not only Kuwaitis but also the large number of foreigners who made up the country's workforce, such as my sister-in-law, Lucy, as well as others in town for short-term business trips. Thousands of innocent people were suddenly caught up in a conflict they didn't see coming and had nothing to do with.

Not letting a good opportunity go to waste, Saddam used these foreigners as a hedge against possible military action against him. His troops took hundreds of hostages and transferred them over the border into Iraq. By late October the Iraqis had taken captive at least 104 Americans and more than 700 British, European, Australian, Japanese, and Kuwaiti men and moved them to as many as seventy strategic sites in Iraq and Kuwait. The hostages were disbursed throughout the country to act as human shields at strategic installations, including military bases, suspected weapons facilities, dams, industrial facilities, and agricultural sites.

My friend Glenn Coleman was one of those human shields. He had been in Kuwait on a three-day business trip to complete a deal to outfit Kuwait Air Force F/A-18 fighter jets with long-range optical cameras. The day of the invasion was supposed to be Glenn's last day in Kuwait. The plan was for Kuwaiti military representatives to sign the purchase agreement in the morning, and Glenn and his team would leave Kuwait on a flight that afternoon.

But instead of boarding a flight to Abu Dhabi (with connecting flights to Europe and the United States), Glenn found himself in the unenviable position of being kidnapped at gunpoint and forced to board a bus headed for Iraq. All the hostages sat in silence as the bus headed north toward the border. The potent smell of gunpowder filled Glenn's nostrils from the muzzle of a recently fired AK-47 positioned inches away from his face, held by one of the guards.

Glenn's head was spinning. He felt as if he was outside himself, like watching a movie he was starring in. He was frozen on the X by circumstances, a wild predicament he never could have imagined. Glenn hadn't been able to complete his business objectives and wasn't returning home to his lovely wife, Hope. He was now a spoil of war, a victim of being in the wrong place at the wrong time.

As the busload of thirty-two recently kidnapped hostages rumbled north toward Iraq, they watched gas fires blazing from oil wells stretched across a desolate, black landscape. As they passed through the northern Rumaila oil field, superheated air blew the fine desert sand in through every open window. The sweaty human bounty sat in silence, their minds racing with fear.

A passage from Dante's *Inferno*, which Glenn had memorized in his high school literature class, popped into his brain: "All hope abandon, ye who enter here." He was surprised by his brain's ability to produce this poetic reference while pondering how truly hopeless he felt in this moment. His straightforward business trip had marked his entry into an in-between that would challenge him to the core. If he was going to get through it, he'd have to reject Dante's warning and hold on to hope no matter what.

Over time, Glenn and the other hostages were split up and moved often, shuttled to various sites, possibly to keep them off-balance, prevent escapes, or make sure no one got too chummy with their Iraqi minders. Glenn spent time in a Basrah prison camp, a uranium-processing facility in al-Qaim (near the Syrian border), a plutonium-enrichment plant near Baghdad, and the al-Tuwaitha nuclear facility.

How do you endure being made a pawn in an international game of brinksmanship? How do you face each day thinking that it might be your last?

If we were told ahead of time how long our layovers in hell would last, they would be so much easier to survive. It's the not knowing that can kill a soul. That's why you *must* take control of whatever you can, even if only your internal dialogue, the thoughts you ruminate on while in the middle of the storm. As World War II concentration camp survivor Viktor Frankl expressed so eloquently in his book *Man's Search for Meaning*:

> We who lived in concentration camps can remember the men who walked through the huts, comforting others, giving away their last piece of bread. They may have been few in number but they offer sufficient proof that everything can be taken from a man but one thing: the last of the human freedoms—to choose one's attitude in any given set of circumstances, to choose one's own way.

Glenn had spent ten years in the navy, some of which were served on submarines. Because of his experience living in small quarters with minimal activities to keep himself occupied outside work shifts, he knew he needed to stay as mentally engaged as possible. He needed to do whatever he could to get off the X of fear and anxiety about the future. A bored mind did not go to good places.

So Glenn wrote poems. He sketched pictures of prisoners and prison guards. He drew cartoons. He discussed and documented ideas of how to communicate and interact with the group's minders. He made lists of items they wanted to negotiate for, such as toilet paper and warmer clothes when the seasons changed. Glenn even designed games for the prisoners to play, including a version of Monopoly that he humorously dubbed "Monotony."

To pass the time, he and several others found ways to exercise, play bridge, tend to plants, and catch rats. They organized themselves into groups, sketched the facilities where they were being held, and came up with ideas of how to escape if the opportunity presented itself. Day after day they did their best to control what they could and maintain faith that they would emerge from this desert purgatory.

Some of the prisoners did not adopt a survival mindset. Overcome by their forced confinement, they isolated themselves from everyone else. They rarely got out of bed or left the sleeping quarters. They checked out. As a result, these individuals were not only more downcast and depressed, but they also got physically sicker than the others. They withered on the vine of uncertainty.

To be fair, the whole world was speculating what Saddam would do, and most of us were not optimistic that he would release the hostages. Everyone feared that he would kill them or they'd be caught in the crossfire once Operation Desert Storm commenced on January 15, 1991—a deadline the Iraqis and their hostages were aware of.

After four and a half months of interminable days, endless boredom, and uninformed speculation about what was happening in the outside world, the hostages were told by their minders that they were about to be released. The Iraqis fed the group their last meal of fish and beer while the prisoners wondered whether they were being lied to and manipulated. To their utter relief, the very next day the hostages boarded an aircraft for their journey home. Against all odds, 156 American hostages returned to the United States on December 10, 1990.

Glenn explained what he learned from this painful experience:

> Make sure that you take full responsibility for the conduct of your life, so that you can have that reconciliation with yourself in the end. . . . Beyond that fundamental finding, my four-and-a-half-month sojourn became an opportunity to discover that an individual's freedom is, by and large, the most important possession known to man.

Adopting a gritty, never-give-up attitude enabled Glenn to endure his captivity and develop the internal fortitude to face what followed. In the decades since his imprisonment, Glenn has battled thyroid, bladder, kidney, prostate, and bone cancers. The cancers are likely a result of his month and a half imprisonment at the al-Tuwaitha nuclear facility, which was bombed by Iran in 1980 and Israel in 1981. At the time of my interviews with Glenn, he was eighty-seven years old and in hospice. Even then, he told me that he was "still getting off the X." Despite the circumstances of failing health, nothing could take away his gratitude for each day or spoil his eternal optimism. May we all have a bit of that fighting spirit, the stubbornness to hold on tight no matter what.

Faith isn't faith unless you can cling to it when circumstances suggest you do otherwise, as Glenn did. I call it *stupid faith*—faith that is stubborn beyond measure, that hangs on when everyone else folds. Stupid faith demands that you never give up. Stupid faith holds on come hell or high water or the flaming desert sky. It is what we need to survive our sojourns on this earth. There will always be difficulty; what makes the difference is what we do in those times of struggle.

While we may not have agency over our circumstances, we have agency over our minds. And though it's not easy to endure the suffering we encounter in life or the dreaded in-betweens, we must do everything we can to remain engaged, surround ourselves with a supportive crew, and do whatever is necessary to lift our spirits and feed our souls.

POSTURE OF GRATITUDE

It is only human to feel as if you might drown in the waves of the in-between, but if you can work your mind into a position of gratitude for that which you *do* have, you take back some control. Gratitude helps you look past the circumstances and imagine that they can be redeemed, that something good can come out of something terrible.

Developing a posture of gratitude in the midst of the mess feels unnatural and even ridiculous. Whenever I think I can't possibly find a reason to be grateful for difficult situations, I think of Dutch national and concentration-camp survivor Corrie ten Boom. She and her family were sent to the Nazi death camps for hiding Jewish families in their home in Amsterdam.

After being trucked to Germany's Ravensbrück camp and taken to the barracks, Corrie discovered that the bunks were covered in fleas. They had taken over the bedding and were feasting on the women's flesh as they tried to sleep. This reality, on top of all the death and destruction in their midst, felt like the straw that would break the camel's back.

But in the midst of that suffering, Corrie's sister Betsie decided that the best way through the inhumane circumstances was to find reasons to be grateful. It's a biblical concept ("in everything give thanks," see 1 Thessalonians 5:16-18); even modern psychology and behavioral studies recognize the power of gratitude. But this concept isn't easily applied in life. To say that it would be difficult to develop an attitude of gratitude in a concentration camp is quite the understatement. Yet Betsie worked to apply this concept to her immediate circumstances. She thanked God for the blessing of being assigned to the same camp as her sister, the miracle of Corrie's ability to smuggle a Bible into the camp, and the fleas.

This last bit of gratitude was too much for Corrie to swallow, and as a reader of her biography *The Hiding Place*, I initially could not abide by it either. How could fleas ever be a good thing? What a silly and even flippant thing to say. Yet Corrie and Betsie eventually learned that the Nazi soldiers refused to go near the barracks because of the fleas. This was the one place the women were safe from beatings and torture. The barracks were also the place they could hear the sisters read from the Bible, sing hymns, and openly pray—all of which tremendously lifted the women's spirits.

Whenever I face difficult situations, I tell myself, *You've got to thank God for the fleas*. Sometimes it's difficult to imagine a silver lining, and yet working to adopt this mental and spiritual posture is life-changing. And the mental flip actually changes you physically. As you feel or express gratitude, your brain chemistry changes with the release of dopamine and serotonin (natural antidepressants). Not allowing the gunk to get you down and finding ways to overcome its deleterious effects also shifts your neural networks. The more you press out of the pain and into a posture of openness and gratitude, your neural network is rewired. It's easier to think positive thoughts and more possible to focus on the light at the end of the tunnel.

But getting there isn't easy. It takes energy to overcome well-worn circuitry that homes in on the bad stuff. The more we endeavor to find the flip, the easier it becomes to move from a crisis mentality to that of a survivalist, and then onto a place where we can thrive again. Do whatever you can to move that needle and make space for a spiritual redemption of circumstances.

What difficulty or irritant does the "flea" represent in your life right now? Can you entertain the idea of a flip, the possibility that something positive and transformative can emerge from this challenge? How might you feed your mind, body, and spirit with goodness and gratitude for what's certainly on the way?

WAR ZONES, REST, AND A CHANGE OF SCENERY

When Joseph and I were based in Iraq, you could always tell when someone was nearing their R&R—a two- or three-week break away from the war zone. Staff members became edgy, angering easily and exploding for minor reasons. The stress was cumulative and unavoidable, fueled by daily adrenaline surges and cortisol dumps when the shelling forced us to jump into bunkers at all hours of the day.

Staff could take advantage of three R&Rs during the Baghdad tour. At the three- or three-and-one-half-month mark, our irritability index began to soar. When a colleague "had a moment" and lost his cool, we'd whisper in hushed tones, "Somebody is due for his R&R."

The amount of work and the nature of that work—trying to save lives—was demanding beyond measure, taking tremendous physical and emotional tolls. Therefore, we were grateful for the R&Rs, happily leaving Baghdad every few months to return to the United States or travel around Europe. These pauses in our work boosted our mental health.

I don't think that regular life is all that different. We need mental breaks. And when we are trying to get off the X, we need even more positive stimuli to counteract the stress of trying to plot and execute the next move. In the age of instant gratification, waiting for your door to open can feel interminable, as can trying to reorient yourself when life-altering circumstances throw you for a loop.

So how can you cope? How is it possible to survive the space between the hurt and the hope? You get out of the war zone in your head. In addition to expressing gratitude, proactively choose to do the opposite of what you feel.

Don't climb into bed and isolate yourself. Instead, connect with friends and family who lift you up. Spend time with people who make you smile. Read books that lift your spirit. Listen to music that makes you dance. Watch documentaries of people who have triumphed over their struggles. Create a gratitude notebook or prayer journal. Put down your devices to take a walk, smell the fresh air, and meditate on the beauty of nature. Work out to elevate your health and flood your brain with endorphins. Feed your soul. Do whatever makes your heart sing.

I generate great ideas when I'm running on the treadmill, taking a walk, or listening to good music. But I also explore new interests. Learning Arabic and traveling to the Middle East added up to more than simply having a good time for me; I was also expanding my knowledge and gathering intelligence for my next steps.

Your chosen activities will abate the negativity and bad feelings, but within them also lies the currency of breakthroughs. Just as rest and recovery are integral to the endurance of world-class long-distance runners, so changing up your scenery lays the groundwork for unique ideas to emerge.

In Frans Johansson's seminal work *The Medici Effect*, he quoted corporate strategist Orit Gadiesh on the value of giving your brain a break, and how that break can affect your long-term output. "You have to be willing to 'waste time' on things that are not directly relevant to your work because you are curious," Gadiesh noted. "But then you are able to, sometimes unconsciously, integrate them back into your work."[14]

Emory University neuroscientist Gregory Berns has offered similar advice about the effects of novelty on the brain in his book *Iconoclast*, noting that "epiphanies rarely occur in familiar settings."[15]

Therefore, when you determine to get off the X, you are committing yourself to living counterculture. You are committing yourself to developing a mindset that goes against your natural inclinations.

But bear in mind: This is no easy road. This battle of the mind will often feel like an emotional roller coaster as you grapple with *the wait*. The struggle isn't bad—it's necessary.

Rest when you're weary. Take breaks when you've hit your limit. Explore different activities and see how they not only bring refreshment but also introduce opportunities to get off the X.

What is one way you might change your scenery today, to refresh yourself and escape the war zone in your head?

PART 5: COUNTERMEASURES FOR THE IN-BETWEENS

We cannot bring the vision to fulfillment through our own efforts, but must live under its inspiration until it fulfills itself.

—Oswald Chambers, *My Utmost for His Highest*

A countermeasure is anything—actions, procedures, or techniques—that effectively negates or mitigates an adversary's ability to exploit your vulnerabilities. The quicker you can employ countermeasures, the less vulnerable you and your systems will be.

CHAPTER SEVENTEEN
THE DESERT ROAD

I must hold in balance the sense of the futility of effort and the sense of the necessity to struggle; the conviction of the inevitability of failure and still the determination to "succeed"—and, more than these, the contradiction between the dead hand of the past and the high intentions of the future.

—F. Scott Fitzgerald, *The Crack-Up*

The minivan full of college students rumbled along at breakneck speed. Edward navigated the uneven highway with its bumps and ditches as if it were my old Disney favorite Mr. Toad's Wild Ride.* The overburdened tires—weighted down with sixteen people, carry-ons, and piles of luggage tied to the roof—kicked up quite a sandstorm. A dust cloud a half-mile long hung in the air behind us as we bounced down the road.

The hot Egyptian air blew through the open windows, sandblasting our faces. The fine dust particles mixed with our perspiration felt grimy and gross, but closing the windows was no option: the air conditioner wasn't working. With outside temperatures

---

*Mr. Toad's Wild Ride was one of Disney World's original attractions, a beloved feature of the park from its opening in October 1971 through September 1998.

hovering around 114 degrees, it was either melt inside a moving sweat lodge or eat dust. We preferred to eat dust.

We were on our way to Port Said on the northern coast, which took about ten hours on the Desert Road. We'd left before dawn, trying to beat the worst heat of the day, but still there was no escaping the scorching sun.

As my head bounced continually against the window, I tried to rest. I desperately missed home: the lovely, lush green state of Florida. I would never take for granted air conditioners again, or anything green for that matter.

The landscape was straight out of *National Geographic* magazine, with boulders scattered over the ground and tan-and-copper-colored mountains that punctuated the bright blue horizon for 360 degrees. Had these places ever been touched by human hands? The pristine nature of it all blew my mind. Every now and then a wild camel or two wandered along in the distance. Other than these hardy creatures, the desert seemed devoid of life.

As I contemplated the extreme landscape, a small black blob appeared on the horizon, slowly coming into focus as we approached: a human being! As our eyes adjusted, we could make out an old woman wrapped in black, standing by herself on the side of the road. There was no chair, no shelter, no bags, no nothing. She stood there quiet and diminutive, with a handbasket hanging on her arm.

As Edward abruptly brought the minivan to a stop, we peered out the window at the old, well-wrinkled woman sporting just a few teeth. Why had he stopped? Maybe she needed help.

Edward exchanged words with her in Arabic and, at the conclusion of the exchange, handed her money. She reached into her basket, pulled out little green cucumbers, and passed them to Edward through the open window. Cucumbers? We could now see that her handbasket was full of them. She was in the middle of the Egyptian desert all by herself selling cucumbers.

I couldn't see any other humans, vehicles, or abodes anywhere on the horizon. Absolutely no traces of civilization. Where had she come from? How long would she stand there for? Who in their right minds would drop their grandma in the middle of the desert to sell cucumbers? Her presence in that desolate place baffled me—so much so that I remember that tiny, gap-toothed Bedouin woman more than thirty years later.

Seeing her on the side of the road enveloped by the grandeur and mystery of that parched environment made me recall the Old Testament story of the Israelites wandering the desert after escaping the clutches of Pharaoh. Were they wandering in a place like this? I assumed so. This was the Egyptian desert after all. Never had I been so close to a biblical story in all my life.

In addition to that ten-hour drive (which felt like eternity to an eighteen-year-old with heatstroke), I have found myself stuck in the desert many times. I've wandered many a lonely stretch, desperately trying to find my way to the land flowing with milk and honey. Sometimes I have no idea where I want to go—my destination a huge question mark. Other times I know where I want to go, but no matter what I try, I can't seem to get there.

I call these periods when you're neither here nor there the *dreaded in-betweens*. These are the dry desert places you experience when you've done everything to move yourself forward but nothing appears to be happening. You've worked valiantly to get off the X, but to no avail. You've applied to every job opportunity but cannot get hired. You've tried out but can't make the team. You've built up the courage to repeatedly put yourself out there, only to be met with silence or rejection.

When you can't figure out how to move yourself forward, the little voice inside your head tries to process what's happening: *Maybe you're not smart enough. Maybe you don't have the right personality or the right skills. Or maybe you're not trying hard enough. Other people are moving forward, why can't you? Maybe you've simply missed the boat and are doomed to a life of unhappiness and failure.*

The maelstrom of uncertainty threatens your very being and you second-guess your hopes for the future.

When I have looked back on those periods of my life when I applied every methodology for getting off the X but still found myself in the in-betweens, hindsight has revealed some incredible truths—specific reasons why I had to wait for certain opportunities to open up.

What if, for all of us, the dreaded in-betweens aren't punishments or failures but critical way stations? What if the time we spend there contains purpose and meaning? Would that make the wait more tolerable?

When we're lying motionless in the desert drained by the heat of the midday sun, and it feels as though nothing is happening, is that perception reality?

UNSEEN REALITIES

Toward the beginning of my career journey, I believed that the circumstances in front of my face were what mattered. I pinned my hopes on the outcomes of certain events, and when they fell through, I panicked. But as I meditated on my situation, I started to wonder whether perception was reality. Was the closed door the end of it? Or was it just the beginning? Was the material world the *only* world? Or was there a better, more accurate way to view my predicaments?

I didn't have the requisite knowledge to forge a meaningful path of my own or redeem beauty from the chaos of difficulty and outright rejection. So I decided to lean on a greater force. If God created me, then he had a special path in mind for me (and everyone else). I gave space to the idea that humans are purpose-built to accomplish our missions, and eventually these missions will be fulfilled at the appropriate time.

Over the years this built up a hope within that sustained me when I didn't know where the rough road would lead, or when I felt strung out waiting for the next steps to materialize.

I repeatedly tested this idea and found that my trust was not misplaced. Fascinating things happened when I challenged my perception of the in-betweens. When it felt as if nothing good was happening, could I trust that God was setting the stage for something bigger and better? Sure enough, before rising doubt or confusion could drown me, clarity of path or purpose would emerge. If I could tread water long enough, the sea would part and expose an opportunity that I had never conceived. I knew this wasn't just a coincidence.

Suffering can take you down or it can transform you. Resist the temptation to fold; consider, instead, whether you can trust that a greater hand is at work. You might be amazed by what's on the horizon that eventually comes into view.

VITAL PREPARATION

It's helpful to point out that during the seemingly interminable waiting at the start of my career, I was being prepared for what came next. Though I felt lost, I maintained a posture of openness and a desire to learn as much as I could from my circumstances. Instead of decrying the fact I was "only" an administrative assistant at an international-aid organization, I soaked up the Capitol Hill environment like a sponge.

I learned how critical advocacy was to relief and development work. I learned the art of diplomacy, how to formulate a position and communicate it quickly and clearly to policymakers and their staff. I learned how to obtain difficult-to-get appointments for foreign aid assistance—for Rwandans after the genocide, Palestinians living in the West Bank, starving North Koreans, and HIV orphans in Uganda.

I accompanied colleagues to congressional offices, the State Department, and foreign embassies to learn how to speak to leaders in various positions of power. I worked with brilliant professionals who specialized in child-survival programs, community-development initiatives, health programs, and grant writing. I started to build my knowledge of a foreign language, taking night classes in Arabic.

On paper, the majority of my job involved answering phones, filing paperwork, and scheduling meetings for others. Yet what I learned in that humble position shaped the quality of my future interactions with foreign intelligence officers, diplomats, presidents, and prime ministers.

The postmodern world places the altar of ego above all else. It tells us to demand attention and push for a higher rank. It proffers that the development of our identity is more important than the development of our expertise.

I am here to argue the opposite. Think less about striving for position and more about giving, serving, and enriching your mind no matter what your station. Even if my twenty-four-year-old ego was bruised by my inability to move forward, I can now see that this time was rich in growth and vital to my future. The incredible amount of knowledge I gained would blossom throughout my career as I brought it to bear on my international intelligence and consulting careers.

What vital things can you do right now, wherever you are, to fill the void of achievement or seeming lack of momentum? What ways can you enrich your mind, absorb new ideas, or unearth new skills to survive your desert space?

CHAPTER EIGHTEEN

DEAD ENDS

The challenge is to find the doors that are clearly marked with an Enter sign and avoid the pain caused by butting our heads against the ones that are shut tight.

—Jack Barsky, *Deep Undercover*

Rejection, unfulfilled dreams, missed opportunities, unexpected losses—these are some of the most achingly difficult situations we deal with as humans. They don't just cause psychological grief or emotional reactions. Our brains register these inputs as physical pain. This neurowiring exists to help us avoid situations that could put us in harm's way. But this protective instinct could also trip us up when we're trying to get off the X, because our brains unconsciously register the notion that taking risks is dangerous: "Stop trying. This hurts!"

But as we know, life is filled with dead ends of every stripe. Our ability to navigate these realities and manage our responses is critical to surviving the in-betweens.

The best way I have found to deal with painful challenges is to push an alternative cognitive response: to reframe. Could a closed door actually be the opposite—a blessing in disguise? If you can entertain the possibility that the loss or rejection will be for your good in the long run, that very act might transform your outlook and expectations. If closed doors and rejection are consequences of taking risks, then we need to get better at managing our responses to the paths not meant for us.

PAUL AND KELSEY'S STORY: BUILD IT BETTER

The sixty-acre resort nestled on six hundred acres of beautiful North Florida terrain looked like the perfect event venue, a place of restoration and rejuvenation. The facility, with its sixty guest rooms, could host youth groups, weddings, concerts, corporate meetings, and church camps. Paul and Kelsey Tompkins had the idea of acquiring and further developing the property, so they pitched their vision to an organization with which they had volunteered a substantial amount of their time. The organization's leadership immediately caught their vision. After acquiring additional investors, the couple negotiated an excellent price and successfully managed the acquisition and development of the land.

Soon thereafter, Paul and Kelsey were asked to run the resort. In November 2015, the newlyweds moved onto the property and helped with everything from marketing and changing beds to organizing the dining rooms and managing meals. Each day drowned in a thousand details as the couple and their small staff hosted a dizzying turnover of guests. As they logged eighty- to ninety-hour workweek, they could barely keep their heads above water. But they believed they were building something important, so the personal sacrifice was worth it.

Not long after they jumped in, however, Paul and Kelsey realized they were being sidelined—engaged in the day-to-day oversight but left out of larger decision-making. This change of roles and amendment of expectations deeply disappointed them, but they were still passionate about what they did, so they continued.

Over time, Paul started hearing of changes on the horizon, whisperings that the organization was interested in taking the property and services in a different direction. So he spoke to the CEO: "I understand you may be making some changes with the property, which is fine. Please just give us a heads-up if this is what you're thinking, so we can make appropriate arrangements on our end."

The CEO demurred, saying that of course they would let Paul and Kelsey know if things changed. He added that regardless of whatever decisions were made, the organization still needed someone to run it. Paul and Kelsey would absolutely stay on.

Weeks passed, and Paul couldn't shake the feeling that major changes were underway but weren't being communicated to them. Each time Paul reached out to leadership to get an update, he was told not to worry.

Then, in March 2017, Paul and Kelsey were called to meet with the CEO. They were told, "We're taking things in a new direction. Today is your last day of work."

Just like that, Paul and Kelsey were fired without cause.

In complete shock, all they could think was, *What do we do now?* The very people who had found the property, pitched the idea, negotiated the successful acquisition, and run its operations were discarded. Without warning, they were left jobless *and* homeless. And this by an organization that purported to care about people's spirits, souls, and spiritual well-being.

Paul and Kelsey knew they would have a hard time buying a house or renting an apartment because neither had a job or income, or even health insurance. This highly motivated and extremely passionate couple had landed squarely and abruptly on the X by circumstances completely outside their control.

Running face-first into a dead end is emotionally jarring. And not knowing what comes next is terrifying. If we can manage to hang on, however, dead ends might be the vehicles by which we find the paths we're meant to travel. If we can summon the strength to look up from the pit we land in to see that the sun is still shining and that the God of all resources can make a way, then we make space for something wonderful to materialize. The act of surrender is so powerful because it acknowledges that bad can be redeemed by good if we wait in hopeful anticipation for this transformation to occur.

That's what Paul and Kelsey did. They prayed, and despite the whirlwind of emotions, they felt an underlying peace. And while praying, Paul thought he heard the words "Wait thirty days." This directive seemed odd, because Paul and Kelsey's family and friends were hours away in Jacksonville. It made the most financial sense to return to Jacksonville and stay there until they could find a place to live.

Despite this logic, the feeling that they should stay in place was strong. If God wanted them to wait, they would wait. Perhaps the next piece of the puzzle was about to be revealed.

Before Paul and Kelsey had married, Paul had served in the Marines, worked as a Florida state trooper for ten years, and spent two years in Afghanistan as a private contractor. He helped train the Afghan National Police and did community liaison work, which took him off base six days a week. In the course of that liaison work, he was badly injured by a vehicle-borne improvised explosive device (VBIED, or car bomb).

After Paul returned to the United States, his lawyers worked to get him a settlement for his injuries, but the process stretched out for six years. Incredibly enough, mere days after Paul and Kelsey were fired from the resort, a final settlement was offered. This unexpected win materialized at just the right time. Paul and Kelsey could afford to put food on the table and get back on their feet.

Over the course of the next few weeks, Paul and Kelsey engaged in many conversations about their lives, knowing that they needed to reevaluate *everything*. The process helped them realize how much they loved real estate: finding diamonds in the rough, negotiating for them, and turning them into something bigger and better.

Paul and Kelsey soon reconnected with an investor friend and went to work. Starting with a few smaller properties, they went on to build a multimillion-dollar real estate investment firm that fixes and flips homes, manages rentals, remodels properties, and builds new construction. Not only are they financially successful, but they also constantly look for ways to serve the community, mentor others, and give to those in need.

Thankfully; Paul and Kelsey's in-between didn't last long. But it was long enough for them to recalculate where they were going and what they were meant to do. Being fired landed them on the X, but they used the X to recalibrate. What felt like an enormous loss turned into a key pivot point.

Dead ends don't have to be stopping places, and rejections don't have to be the arbiter of your future potential. As Paul and Kelsey did, take your time on the X to make critical decisions that will propel you to the place you need to be. Now that's the ultimate flip!

CHAPTER NINETEEN

THE OPERATIONAL HOLD

Enthusiasm is common. Endurance is rare.

—Angela Duckworth, *Grit: The Power of Passion and Perseverance*

Waiting is hard.

Our global digital culture has rewired our brains to dislike anything that feels like a pause, because waiting makes us feel as if we are out of control. Delayed gratification—which used to be part and parcel of progress—now feels like antiprogress and anathema to success. Any strategy that doesn't deliver immediate results, answers, or solutions is no strategy at all.

Or is it?

When I look back on my life, I can clearly see how critical the wait was. The moments when I felt most stuck and unable to program my way off the X were the moments when the most important chess moves were being made in my favor. Unbeknownst to me, the most critical pieces of the puzzle were being moved into position for my benefit. Waiting wasn't wasted time. The moments full of doubt and despair were not a jail sentence but an operational hold.

This strategic waiting period is full of activity we cannot always see. Various pieces of the puzzle need time to align. Though we might feel the urge to do so, we can't rush the process. We have to wait patiently, pressing into an inner faith that whispers, *I know it hurts, but don't give up.*

The operational hold releases its treasures to those with the perseverance to wait for the longed-for opportunities and direction. As the popular saying goes, "God is never late."

CURVEBALLS AND REDIRECTION

My path into the CIA was not easy or straightforward. While finishing up my second and final year in my master's program at Georgetown University, I received a conditional offer of employment from the CIA to serve as a leadership analyst in the Directorate of Analysis. I was the first person in my graduating class at the Center for Contemporary Arab Studies to land a job. The director of the career center was so proud. He gave me a Georgetown mug to congratulate me and mark the occasion. I loved that mug. And I graduated with great joy knowing that I was about to slide into one of the coolest jobs on the planet. For the first time in my life, something had come easily.

A couple of weeks later and just days before I was to kick off my career, I received a strange letter in the mail from the CIA. For reasons they did not provide, the analyst position was abruptly and unceremoniously rescinded. Quicker than I could snap my fingers, this amazing job and the career of a lifetime was pulled right out from under me. I was in shock.

I'd gone from being the first to land a job to being the last woman standing, the only graduate in my program who had *not* gotten a job. Every few weeks after the job fell through, the director of the career center would call to find out whether I'd found employment. He was desperate to close the books and declare to Georgetown leadership that all grads in the program were good to go. I was holding them back from this proud declaration. I was affecting the School of Foreign Service's bottom line, the amount of time they could advertise that it took their graduates to secure employment. I wondered whether the career center wanted its mug back.

When I finally did acquire a job, it was beyond embarrassing: temp work as a secretary for an international development organization on Capitol Hill. I was beside myself. Why did I just spend two years of my life studying day and night and going into debt to take a temp job that required only a high school degree? This was not my calling in life, but for the love of God, what was? Why could I not figure that out? What in the world was wrong with me?

As I explained extensively in my first book, *Breaking Cover*, sometimes you have to wait so that another opportunity—the one you're supposed to take—is revealed to you. In cases like this, rejection isn't meant to define your overall capabilities; it's the instrument used to prevent you from heading in the wrong direction. What feels like a tragedy is actually a blessing, though in the moment it feels like a slap in the face.

The forced redirection of my career trajectory was critical: if I'd begun work as an analyst at the CIA, I could not have served in the agency as an undercover agent. Once a person is hired into the CIA, it is almost impossible to change directorates, to transfer from analysis into operations. I had no idea that I was on the wrong track, not meant to be an analyst and spend my career at CIA headquarters in Langley. I was meant to be an operator and live abroad. My personality was far more suited to that of an intelligence collector than a leadership analyst.

That road was closed for a purpose. Not only did I need time to discover the "other" side of the CIA, but I also needed to enter the recruitment process at just the right time. Despite all the pain and uncertainty of the whiplash, I found myself standing on the precipice of an intelligence career that would take me to the Middle East for the majority of the next ten years.

Because of that, I would receive the best counterterrorism schooling in the world: I dealt with terrorists and terror sources face-to-face. I participated in the collection of intelligence to prevent car bombs from blowing up, improvised explosive devices from exploding, and troops from entering booby-trapped buildings. I also had the chance to save Iraqi civilians from being tortured and killed by al-Qaeda operatives they would not support.

When my background investigation was completed in early fall 2001 and I was added to the January 2002 roster of recruits, passenger planes commandeered by terrorists hit the World Trade Center, the Pentagon, and a field in Shanksville, Pennsylvania. The world changed on a dime, and I was right there, perfectly prepared and ready to enter service at one of the most crucial moments in US history.

When life throws curveballs, we humans tend to interpret these developments in the worst possible light. We have a hard time imagining how painful moments could ever bring us to a better place. So here's the great challenge: Instead of letting interpretation bias serve as our crystal ball, can we create some space in the middle of the pain for the opposite? Can we give space to a God who knows our capabilities, purposes, and potential better than we do? Can we consider that we might need to learn, grow, or make adjustments to our course to prepare us for the next big thing?

When it seems you've done all you can and nothing is happening, you've got to stubbornly hang in there. If you can entertain the possibility that something amazing is waiting on the other side of your pain, you can survive the in-betweens.

You don't know what's around the next corner.

LILLIAN'S STORY: UNCERTAIN PATH AND PURPOSE

Lillian Trasher sat helplessly on her bed, tears streaming down her face. She didn't understand the flood of emotion spilling out of her, the feeling of being turned inside out.

What's wrong with me?, she thought.

Earlier that night, Lillian had accompanied a friend to their small church in Marion, North Carolina, to hear an American missionary talk about life and service in India. Comfortably settled in the pew, Lillian listened to the woman explain what it was like to live abroad and serve others in a country far from home. Her stories were arresting, full of faith and intrigue.

As Lillian sat glued to the presentation, something strange happened. The longer the missionary spoke, the more Lillian felt unsettled. What began as an almost imperceptible stirring grew stronger and stronger until the rest of the room faded into the background and Lillian could no longer concentrate on what the woman was saying.

Despite her best efforts to remain in control, her eyes welled up and tears rolled down her face. The sudden inability to moderate her emotions startled her. As the service concluded, all she could think was, *I have to get out of here.*

Lillian carefully got up and politely excused herself. As she walked back to the orphanage where she had been working for the past two years, she could barely breathe, conscious that only a weak veneer held back what felt like a dam about to burst.

Safely ensconced in her small, simple room, the twenty-two-year-old wept uncontrollably for hours. And in the midst of this strange internal explosion, Lillian seemed to gain a life-altering understanding: all that *was* would not *be* any longer. She did not know how or why, but she came to understand that God was calling her to Africa. This calling was strong and completely bewildering. The idea about serving abroad had bounced around in her head for some time, but in this moment she knew that it wasn't "possibly" or "someday." It was *now*. Lillian was called to serve in an unknown capacity, somewhere on the giant continent of Africa.

This was crazy. How could it be? In ten days Lillian was set to marry the love of her life, Tom Jordan.* She'd designed and sewn her wedding dress. All preparations for the big day were complete. And now this? The timing of this calling was deeply inconvenient in the face of an impending wedding. Lillian knew that Tom wasn't called to missions work abroad. They had talked about this kind of service in the past, and he was disinterested in such a course of action. How would Tom respond to this jarring news?

Lillian's thoughts then turned to her family and friends. Would they support her? Would they assume she'd gone mad? How could she drop this bombshell when she didn't have an explanation for what she would do, where she would go, or how she would make it happen. This unexpected change in plans and direction would challenge both Lillian's and society's conception of the course of a young woman's life in turn-of-the-century America.

This is overwhelming. Where do I begin? she wondered.

Lillian started with the most painful part: talking to Tom. He was quite generous in his response. He was more than happy to wait for Lillian for a year or two, and then they would get married.

But deep down, Lillian knew that she could not continue with their engagement. Tom didn't feel any pull to the mission field, and Lillian had a feeling this wouldn't be a short-term expedition. Heartbroken by it all, Lillian and Tom canceled the wedding. Without warning, their lives were headed in two separate directions.

---

*Lillian's fiancé is referred to in most literature as Tom Jordan, except in the book *Lillian Trasher: The Greatest Wonder in Egypt*, where he is referred to as Tom Goodson.

Lillian's family was deeply shocked. It was not proper for a young woman to call off a wedding to go off on her own, not knowing what she would do. They could not bless such a confounding proposition.

Despite her family's disapproval, Lillian felt a strange pull to a particular course of action: travel to a missionary conference in Pittsburgh, Pennsylvania, and wait for the next step to be revealed. *Just get to Pittsburgh, and the rest will work itself out*, Lillian thought.

Lillian's friends helped raise money to send her to the conference. When the ten dollars would get her only to Washington, DC, Lillian figured she'd trust God for the rest.

It must have been intimidating to travel alone from North Carolina to the nation's capital in 1910. When she arrived at the address given her for a night's stay, the host, Miss Olivier, said, "My house is full. I am entertaining a missionary family from Egypt. But, please, come in and join us for lunch."

When seated at the table, Lillian met Reverend Brelsford and his wife. As soon as he learned of Lillian's intentions to travel to Africa, Reverend Brelsford queried, "You don't have the backing of a church or the sponsorship of a mission board, your family doesn't support you, you're alone, and you have no money? And, to top it off, you have no clarity about where you want to go and what you want to do?"

This was not how missions worked, he repeated. What a naive young lady to think she was capable of engaging in such complicated matters as foreign missions, and then to try to do it on her own. As Reverend Brelsford chided her, Lillian felt the weight of his condescending tone, and she shrank with embarrassment. Her intentions did, indeed, sound foolish. Maybe she hadn't heard from God.

One of the rooms at Miss Olivier's opened up that night, making it possible for Lillian to stay as a guest. She was so crushed by the vagueness and uncertainty of it all that she cried herself to sleep.

The next morning, when Lillian encountered Reverend Brelsford in the sitting room, she braced herself. What came next shocked her. He said, "I must confess I was hasty. Can you forgive me for doubting your call? It's just that it was so shocking to think that a young girl such as you would dare to venture out to the other side of the world without her family or money or other arrangements. We are used to doing things in an orderly manner, and it just seemed preposterous to us. However, God does work in mysterious ways, and we can see that you have faith."[16]

Next, Reverend Brelsford made a surprising offer. He said that if Lillian could make her way to Egypt, she could work at the mission house in Assiout in exchange for room and board. Despite the awkwardness between them, this offer struck her as one she should accept. No other options had materialized, so Lillian reasoned that this was a good next step. She would eventually book a ticket for a transatlantic voyage on the steamship SS *Berlin* to Alexandria, Egypt, departing October 8, 1910.

Lillian's anxiety grew as she faced numerous financial challenges days before her departure.

As she waited for her sister Jennie to arrive in New York City to accompany her to Africa, she realized the entire trip might be in jeopardy. She still required the money to pay for the steamship booking. In fact, nothing about this journey had been easy. Every time she had solved a problem, her efforts were thwarted by another set of challenges. Were these obstacles a sign that she had been wrong all along?

As Lillian grew sick with worry and dread, a woman she had never met showed up at her door. The woman was there to give her an incredible $60 for her trip.* This was the last piece of the puzzle, the final payment she required for the voyage.

*In 1910, $60 was equal to approximately $1,800 in 2024.

So Lillian was off, four months after receiving her calling. Three weeks later, Lillian and Jennie arrived at the bustling port city of Alexandria and from there traveled to Reverend Brelsford's Apostolic Faith Mission in Upper Egypt. Lillian focused on studying Arabic and exploring the city, continually praying that her purpose would be revealed to her in due time.

A few months later, on a dark and cold January night, a young Egyptian man showed up at the mission asking for help for a dying woman. Lillian, Egyptian staff member Kamil, and missionary Sela Friend scurried after the stranger, following him into a part of the city Lillian had never seen before. They navigated a dark maze of people, donkey carts, piles of discarded trash, and small hovels. The human misery that enveloped this part of town was palpable and disturbing. Lillian had never seen such poverty before.

After a windy jaunt, they arrived at their destination: a small mud hut close to the Nile. As Lillian's eyes adjusted to the darkness inside, she saw a young woman about fifteen or sixteen years old lying on the floor and an old woman beside her holding a tiny package. When Lillian knelt to take the girl's pulse, the young girl stirred, grabbed her arm, and whispered in Arabic, "Please, please, take her." After uttering this desperate plea, the young woman expelled her last breath.

A strange wail came out of the package on the old woman's lap, and Lillian realized that the odd bundle was a baby. When she unwrapped the filthy swaddling, she found an infant on the edge of death, all skin and bones.

The old woman, possibly the baby's grandmother, pleaded with Lillian to take the child, saying, "I don't know what to do with it." Under her breath she noted, "It's just a girl anyway."

Not wanting to leave the baby alone in that dingy, cramped space where she would surely die, Sela and Kamil reluctantly agreed to let Lillian bring the baby back to the mission. They assumed it was better than leaving the baby to die in the hovel or having her thrown into the Nile, as desperate people sometimes did with unwanted children.

Once back at the mission, the light of the kerosene lamps revealed just how emaciated and sick the child was. She appeared to have been sewn into her clothes, which means there had been no way to change or clean her. At the time, some Egyptians wouldn't bathe a baby until it was forty days old, believing they were protecting it from catching a cold. The tiny infant was caked in filth. Not surprisingly, underneath the putrid garments the baby's flesh was rotting. Saving her would require a miracle.

Lillian and Jennie spent the next few days doing their best to coax drops of milk into the baby's mouth and tend to her wounds. The child's constant anguished cries disturbed the other residents of the mission, who eventually delivered an ultimatum: "You cannot stay here with that sickly child. Go give her back."[17]

Shocked, Lillian asked, "Give her back to whom? There's no one to give her to!"

The mission house leadership didn't care where Lillian took the baby as long as they could get on with their lives. Lillian and Jennie's efforts seemed futile anyway.

With no other options, Lillian made the shocking decision to use the small amount of money she had to rent her own place. If they wouldn't permit her to keep the baby, she'd leave the mission. It was the right thing to do. In fact, it felt like the *only thing* to do.

Lillian's decision to strike out on her own shocked the missionaries, who thought that she was, once again, being incredibly naive. At best she would struggle. She could even starve to death. Furthermore, without the protection of a male guardian, she would be at risk of assault. But Lillian felt deeply in her heart that God had given her this baby, whom she and Jennie named Farida, which means "rare, precious, or one-of-a-kind" in Arabic.

On February 10, 1911, Lillian, Jennie, and baby Farida moved into a small apartment. In the process of saving this dying baby,

Lillian realized what she was meant to do: help the poorest of the poor. This was no strategic decision but the cumulative result of putting one foot in front of the other. She would save desperate street children and those unable to be cared for by their poverty-stricken families.

The rental of that first apartment ushered in the start of a new chapter: the beginnings of an orphanage. Lillian began telling villagers that her vision was to take in children who had lost their parents. Soon thereafter, she was asked to accept a brother and sister, ages four and six. Their parents had just died, and their impoverished uncle couldn't care for them. Five months later, Lillian took in her fourth child, a five-year-old boy named Habib.

Over time, Lillian added more and more children. Provisions were not plentiful, but they trickled in from generous people nearby, from Egyptians in other parts of the country and from donors in Europe and the United States. Lillian and her children didn't have much, but they never missed a meal.

Because of Lillian's willingness to push through every obstacle and not allow fear or uncertainty to stop her, she fulfilled her calling beyond her wildest dreams. Despite disease, financial hardship, the economic strains of World Wars I and II, anti-foreign sentiment during the Egyptian Revolution in 1952, and scores of other difficulties, Lillian and her children survived. Nothing came easy, but nothing worth building ever does.

Lillian had dreamed of raising as many as twelve children. By 1919 she had one hundred children in her care, and that number would swell to twelve hundred.

We often assume that people who do great things in the world have a bevy of secret powers. But what's required is so basic. A couple of months before Lillian passed away, a reporter asked her, "Miss Trasher, what is the secret of your success?"

"There isn't any secret," she replied. "I just stayed. I did not quit."[18]

Our culture is rife with the subconscious message that if something is difficult, it must be wrong. If something pushes us too hard or demands too much from us, it's not the right opportunity. If a person or situation is too difficult to deal with, we should preserve our mental health and remove ourselves from the source of that pain. If you feel anxiety, walk away; if you feel fear, find a safe space. A path filled with obstacles is a sign you're on the wrong path.

Unfortunately, these misguided messages encourage us to give up too soon and see difficulty as anathema to success, when the reality is the opposite: fulfilling your purpose and having a meaningful impact on the world requires great fortitude as a bulwark against the external waves of opposition and the internal tsunamis of doubt that plague us throughout the climb.

MARCHING ORDERS TO NOWHERE

When I left the CIA, I felt a calling to share what I'd learned in that challenging ten-year career to help others grow their capability and confidence. The lessons I'd learned were applicable to men and women in every industry, and if I could help ease someone else's struggle, my own struggle would have been worth it. I was so certain of this spiritual calling that I began to write my first book while still employed by the CIA and had faith that they would eventually permit me to publish it.

I was highly motivated, writing at every opportunity. Thank God I didn't know how long it would take me to get a book written and published. Thank God I didn't know how much rejection would be involved and how many people would give me a strong pass because I was unknown and had no public platform. (Of course I didn't have a platform. I had been off the grid for thirteen years.)

When you look at other peoples' achievements, you see the final products. You don't see what went into birthing them, the failures or difficulties endured along the way. Yet it's critical to deconstruct this process so you can reframe your understanding of what a successful path looks like. If you don't have the proper mindset, you could give up too early. You won't be able to stay on the path as Lillian Trasher did, willing to weather extreme opposition and doubt.

In 2011, I was working full-time at the agency and writing *Breaking Cover* at night and on weekends. After a year or so, however, I realized the monitor wasn't very good. Unsure how to change it, I threw it into the trash. Starting from scratch, I began work on a different kind of manuscript and a thirty-page book proposal to accompany book effort number two. I tried and tried to obtain representation for my book, but no literary agent was willing to take me on. I couldn't get any traction.

Since what I was doing wasn't working, I tried another approach. I secured the services of an experienced publishing consultant to help me position the manuscript and market my product better. I found myself rewriting much of the book to fit her suggested guidelines of what would sell in the market. After weathering dozens more rejections from literary agents, I finally secured representation from an agent in New York City.

My new agent was smart and worked hard, but despite her best efforts, she couldn't get me a book deal. I was still considered too risky. Publishing houses did not want to take a chance on someone unproven. They were so focused on acquiring authors with huge public platforms that they didn't take time to delve in or understand my message or my vision. They didn't take time to gauge my grit. They didn't take time to assess my potential, to see how drive and determination fill every cell of my body.

Publishers are notoriously risk averse and won't invest in a person or their book unless they are a proven quantity. I was a proven quantity only in the shadowy underworld of espionage, not in the shiny literary circles of big cities and famous people. In a world of "platform over person," I would never make it.

At this point I began to wander the desert of weariness and doubt, seemingly walking in circles. For years I literally and figurately lived in deserts, unable to extract myself from the parched environment that made me question everything. Had I misunderstood my calling? Would this book ever happen?

As I lay dazed and confused, wilting in the dreaded in-between, my sister Julie sent me the following excerpt from a blog piece she had just read:

> Your life is not little, and your playing small doesn't serve the world. Your living large, on the other hand—your being your true self despite fear, fatigue, doubt and opposition—will serve the world more than you can imagine. In fact, it may help save it. And saving the world, after all, is what all heroes (including you) are here to do.[19]

I read the passage and exhaled deeply. My faith hung in the balance, but Julie was wise. I needed to trust God that my time in this desert would not last forever. So I continued to wait, pushing down negative, defeatist thoughts. I tried my best to be patient, to keep the faith.

After the passage of another long and unproductive year, a new friend offered to introduce me to his literary agent. After a few weeks I miraculously secured the Austin-based agency's representation. This agent understood me, got my mission, and was 100 percent sold on what I was trying to accomplish. Right as I was about to throw in the towel, my new agent told me how much she believed in me and how certain she was that she could get me a book deal. Could this be it? Was it finally time for this to happen?

Within a few months the elusive promised land came into view. Five long years after starting this endeavor, the impossible was made possible. My book was shopped around and elicited interest from several publishers, and I was finally offered a book deal. Altogether, the process took seven years, three different manuscripts, two literary agents, and a ridiculous amount of second-guessing myself before *Breaking Cover* became a reality.

Now here's the interesting part: There's a reason why I had to wait. There was a purpose for the in-between, and a good one. The last five chapters of the book describe the Herculean effort to find a country willing to accept the group of persecuted Iraqi Christians we were working to save from the ravages of ISIS. I had secured a contract with the literary agency right before this operation occurred, which began in the fall of 2015 and commenced with a miraculous airlift on December 10.

This mission was the culmination of everything Joseph and I had learned working as CIA officers specializing in counterterrorism, counterintelligence, and complex operations in the Arab world. The airlift of 149 Iraqis from Erbil, Kurdistan, to their new home in Slovakia on December 10, 2015, gave critical context to the rest of the material in the book. It was the ultimate demonstration of how purpose and meaning can come from difficulty and suffering.

If the book had come out earlier, I could not have included this incredibly inspiring and life-altering event. My desert experience wasn't a punishment, it was a way station. The dreaded in-between was an operational hold, a pregnant pause required for the other pieces of the complicated puzzle to line up.

I wish I could have known and appreciated that earlier. I would have been less anxious. I would not have been held hostage to a spiritual tug-of-war between hope and despair but instead would have trusted that things *were* moving forward even when I couldn't see it. This lesson has enabled me to view the dreaded in-betweens as opportunities to exercise my faith to believe in things not yet seen instead of allowing the unknown to cause soul-crushing self-doubt or spark an existential crisis.

It's important to recognize when you're on the hamster wheel and can't seem to make progress. Stop running and expending unnecessary energy. If you've done all you can to get off the X and you've employed the penetration-testing methodology to explore alternative ways of achieving your objective, it's time to wait for the pieces of the puzzle to align and to remember whose hands hold them. The results will be more beautiful and better executed than you can imagine.

CHAPTER TWENTY
THE SANDS OF TIME: PERCEPTION VS. REALITY

Though it tarries, wait for it.

—Habakkuk 2:3

When you are waiting anxiously for major developments in your life to move forward, time takes on different attributes. It seems to slow down. When you are trying to get a job, obtain a mortgage, land an important project, earn a spot on the team, or secure an investment for your company, the second hand of the clock seems to tick-tick-tick soooo ssssslowly. You twiddle your thumbs waiting for someone, somewhere to give you good news. The monotony of the minutes marching makes the wait feel so long.

I know this phenomenon well. The period of time between the rejection of the CIA analyst position and the conditional offer of employment to serve in the Directorate of Operations felt like desert wandering that would never end. The trauma from all the rejections was compounded by the fact that I was right back where I started: I had an extra degree and was still unable to get a job. And now I had the added responsibility of repaying large educational loans. No matter how many resumes I sent out and job postings I responded to, I could not induce a positive outcome.

I ran that hamster wheel like a champ, only to get flung off this way and that.

When I look back now to determine how long I spent in the in-between, the best I can deduce is that it lasted less than a year. That realization really surprised me. The period in which I wandered aimlessly in the desert felt as though it had lasted *forever*, but it was only ten to twelve months. Why did it feel so interminable?

Put simply, physical and emotional pain affect the way we experience time. It's called the "time-emotion paradox."[20] In other words, time feels differently depending on the context. Time flies when you're having fun, but pain does the opposite. Pain "dilates time perception" because it increases arousal.[21] Pain grabs our focus and holds it tightly to our bosoms, making us aware of every minute we are unable to gain traction. Our perceived failures beget a bevy of negative emotions that make the hands of time freeze. It's as if we're in a suspended state—neither here nor there. This warped sense of time causes us to feel married to the in-between because we don't know how long this period will last. We worry we'll never emerge from it.

Science has demonstrated that pain and suffering lie to us; our perception of time can't be trusted. But experiments show that when research subjects are explicitly told how long a painful episode will last, they cope better. For example, one study demonstrated that children's tolerance for acute procedural pain and discomfort is increased when they are explicitly told how much time is remaining during the procedure.[22]

A good doctor or nurse is well schooled in this: "You're going to feel a quick pinch," or "This will hurt for just a few seconds." A medical professional whose bedside manner is calm and informative is *everything*. Patients want to be reassured of what's happening to their bodies. It gives them a measure of control over something with so many unknowns.

When I had LASIK to improve my vision, I was grateful to the surgeons and technicians who walked me through each step of the procedure. When my eye was being taped open, I needed to understand how long the lasering process would last and what I would experience in those couple of minutes. That helped me gain mastery over my nerves rather than be convinced I was the subject of medieval torture.

We struggle in the in-betweens because we feel a loss of control over our circumstances or environment. Our postmodern culture leads us to believe that the in-betweens are bad or unusual, but what if this time is not an aberration? What if, instead, it's a necessary part of moving forward in life? What if the in-betweens are sacred waiting spaces or holy holding patterns?

Understanding the purpose of the in-betweens can significantly reduce anxiety associated with the process of getting off the X. Humans spend a great deal of our lives in these spaces, so learning how to manage our expectations is a critical life skill with a direct impact on our mental and emotional health. If we can survive the in-betweens, we can handle the demands of what comes next.

PART 6: AGENTS OF INFLUENCE

To help people find themselves is often to surprise them with new-found joy. . . . It turns out that the more enduring joys are born of an unselfish purpose to serve others.

—Helen Keller, *Light in My Darkness*

An agent of influence is a person of some stature who uses their position to modify discourse, shape public opinion, affect decision-making, and change behavior to produce results beneficial to the agent's organization.

CHAPTER TWENTY-ONE
DANGLES AND DECOYS

Focusing is about saying no.

—Steve Jobs

An interesting phenomenon may occur when you decide to get off the X. Circumstances seem to conspire against you, keeping you from implementing your chosen course of action. This often manifests as the sudden appearance of a different opportunity waved in front of your eyes. In intelligence this is referred to as a dangle or decoy. Like bright shiny objects, dangles and decoys mesmerize and tempt you, but they are not the ideal path.

In the intelligence world this could look like a competing agency sending an operative to draw your attention. The dangle is made to look like an authentic target, the ideal spy you dream of recruiting. The ultimate deception is to make you, the adversary, think that the dangle is the real deal, worthy of recruitment as a source of information. The purpose of a dangle, however, is to position a double agent to collect intelligence about *you*, plant disinformation, and waste your time and resources.

Similarly, a decoy is a type of dangle used to draw you away from a more important and legitimate target. Decoys—whether people, operations, or devices—deflect your attention from the worthier opportunity, wasting your time, emotions, and other resources.

Both dangles and decoys serve as fake representations of the real thing. Paying attention to them can prove devastating if you take your eye off the prize and step away from your intuitive sense of direction or the clear calling on your life.

SETTLE OR SEEK ADVENTURE?

When Joseph and I made the decision to leave the CIA, a flood of other options suddenly materialized. We spent most of our careers going wherever the agency sent us and having few, if any, alternatives. But now we were hitting our stride. As I placed one foot out the door, I was offered three different positions, all of which would have represented a significant leap in my agency career. Furthermore, I could see myself doing those jobs and doing them well. They were juicy leadership roles that I could sink my teeth into and make a difference.

The temptations to stay in the CIA made me feel torn. I had gained so much expertise by serving in difficult places, and these positions would have been my chance to teach others, give back, build a better workplace, and run more effective operations. Yet I knew it was time to go. Deep down I sensed that I was being led outside the intelligence bubble, a scary departure from the stability of a government job. I had no idea how the next steps would materialize. The change of direction required me to exercise my faith and believe in things that did not yet exist. I had to summon the courage to leave enticing opportunities at CIA headquarters for the complete unknown. I was choosing risk over certainty.

At the same time, Joseph was warned by well-respected colleagues, "You'll never feel such purpose again if you retire from agency work. You'll never have the kind of impact on the outside as you do here in the CIA." Those declarations were supported by the experiences of people we knew who had returned to the agency because they didn't have the kind of post-CIA careers they'd hoped for. Being exposed to the most cutting-edge intelligence and carrying out secret operations gave most of us a high that was not easy to replace. Stopping terror attacks before they occur is a mission hard to replicate.

The refrain was "You can't" or "You shouldn't," but we did. It took years to confirm this, but the naysayers were wrong. Most were well intentioned, but they didn't know much about our faith, our fighting spirit, the extent of our skills, or our determination to succeed. Certainly, we would need all these qualities to survive on the outside. We would need a huge dose of stubborn determination to make our way outside the protected and reclusive intelligence sphere.

My good friend and career strategist Jenny Blake explained it well in her book *Pivot: The Only Move That Matters Is Your Next One*. Just when you're ready to get off the X, you will be bombarded with messages suggesting that you take a safer course of action. She calls this phenomenon the "pivot paradox" in which upon deciding to take a risk, you are warned to be careful because "the grass is always greener on the other side."

> Too often this is used as a phrase to keep people in line. . . . The message is to settle, to be happy with what you've got. . . . I once read a book about entrepreneurship that, at every chapter, seemed meant to deter me from actually leaving my job. By the end, it was clear that the author's advice would have been to ditch my greener grass fantasy and continue trucking along at my dependable corporate job.[23]

Why do a bevy of options suddenly appear at the fork in the road to pull us back from the very thing we are meant to do? Why is doubt pitched against us as we summon the courage to make our move?

Jenny's intuitive hunch about her life's direction was right on target. Though the ride has been challenging—as life changes always are—her dream pasture *was* greener. Jenny's consulting business is thriving. She found exactly where she was supposed to be, and all the difficulties she encountered along the way did not deter her. In fact, the challenges she faced were key to her cracking the career-builder code, which she uses to guide others on their journeys.

Since leaving the agency, Joseph and I have had the opportunity to affect countless individuals through the Iraq airlift operation, distribution of my books, hundreds of speaking engagements reaching thousands of people, and the mentoring assistance we invest in others along the way. And, like Jenny's endeavor, our boutique international advisory business is thriving. There is no question in our minds that we made the right decision, and we traveled in the direction of our ultimate purpose, even when dangles and decoys made us second-guess ourselves on the threshold of that major life change.

CHAPTER TWENTY-TWO
CODE BREAKERS

What a revelation! . . . How magnificent to find my life's calling, at long last!

—Julia Child, with Alex Prud'homme, *My Life in France*

When I look back at my life and take stock of all the fear I've harbored over the years, I understand now that most of it was not the fear of a particular thing but general fear of the unknown. I'm grateful that despite this natural inclination to fear, I still jumped into the deep end of the pool. And because I was keenly aware of the limitations of my knowledge and experience, I worked extra hard. I pushed through the pain repeatedly in order to learn and grow. I'm fortunate that my parents inculcated in me the desire to fight, but even if you didn't have a cheerleader in your corner when you were young, you can still learn how to fight. There's no expiration date for learning to push through the fear. As with exercising a muscle, the more you venture into the unknown, the easier it gets. Survival requires concerted effort to keep moving forward no matter what the circumstances.

You cannot thrive without the struggle. It's one of life's great contradictions: we flinch when we face difficulties, but we require them to blossom into someone more capable. You can't do the cool stuff without first marinating in the struggle.

Life would have been so much easier if I had cracked that code earlier. If I'd understood the patterns, I wouldn't have spent so much time battling worry and anxiety. I would have put that energy to better use. I wouldn't have been concerned about lagging behind everyone else. I would have recognized that I was on a different path (and what an extremely interesting one it has turned out to be). The obstacles have done nothing but build strength and capacity, the wisdom that I now share with others. There was no shorter course to run, no quicker way for me to get there.

Now that I'm on the other side of all of that, it delights me to shout from the rooftops, "I've decrypted the cipher! I've broken the code!" I understand and respect the great contradiction: embrace the struggles because they are the vehicles by which we develop our superpowers. The willingness to push off the X and do the hard things is what cultivates wisdom, forges insight, develops expertise, and pushes us through the darkness into the light of progress and achievement.

Those who avoid the hard things tend to wither on the vine. If you do the opposite of what feels good in the moment, and if you are willing to endure short-term pain for a longer-term payout, then you get to walk on the wild side of life. I highly recommend it.

THE ELEVATION EFFECT

We all know how quickly bad news spreads. Bad ideas beget bad ideas, and we are keenly aware of how unfortunate things such as germs and disease disperse like lightning through a population. What is often overlooked is the other side of the spectrum: the powerful reach, contagiousness, and long-term legacy of good works. We are less aware of how helping others improves not only the direct beneficiary but many who bear witness to that investment.

Emotional contagion is defined as a "phenomenon where the observed behavior of one individual leads to the reflexive production of the same behavior by others."[24] Emotional contagion can be spread by body language, such as facial expressions, vocal tone, posture, and movement. And that contagion might spread positive or negative emotions, good feelings or bad.

It turns out that witnessing another person's acts of charity, generosity, kindness, or selflessness causes something called the *elevation effect*—the explosion of motivation to replicate that action, to do something good for another human being. This behavioral response is associated with the hormone oxytocin, which suggests a possible underlying biological mechanism for this reaction.[25]

I believe that seeing someone achieve something significant sparks a desire to dig deeper and reach higher. Once the impossible is made possible by someone in our orbit, we are inspired to up the ante and set higher personal goals.

However you choose to walk in this world, you will cause ripples. When you smile, those around you are more likely to smile and feel happy. When you voice enthusiasm about a project, others will feel more enthusiastic. When you have faith for a positive outcome, you inspire greater amounts of faith in others. When you lift someone's spirit, that person then has the capacity and wherewithal to uplift others in turn.[26]

You have the power to change lives every minute of every day. Your mission, should you choose to accept it, is to become an agent of influence. With your newfound tradecraft in hand, you can help others subvert the deceptive thoughts that threaten to keep them locked in a defensive posture. You can help them push through obstacles, strategize methods of moving forward, survive the dreaded in-betweens, and avoid dangles, decoys, and other choke points. You have all the tools you need to push yourself and others forward.

Our ultimate calling is to be agents of influence, acting as lightning rods to spark good works in others. Enthusiasm is contagious. Faith is fire. And grit and determination are worth more than gold. Personal glory is fleeting. Investing in others launches a legacy.

CHAPTER TWENTY-THREE

A WALK ON THE WILD SIDE

A life not lived for others is not a life.

—Mother Teresa

When Lillian Trasher was poised to travel to the other side of the globe for some unknown purpose, everyone wondered whether she had gone mad. She shattered cultural norms by moving to Egypt and raising children as an unmarried foreign woman with no previous experience in the region. Lillian's willingness to live a hardscrabble existence to care for underprivileged children is the ultimate illustration of getting out of your comfort zone.

But was it the smartest thing to do? Was all the hardship worth it?

By the time Lillian Trasher died in 1961 at age seventy-four, she had provided a loving home for more than ten thousand children, widows, and blind women. Despite the warnings that she shouldn't or couldn't do this, Lillian defied everyone's expectations. The naive young woman from a small town in America painstakingly built and ran the largest orphanage in Egypt. More than one hundred years later, that orphanage still exists. The Lillian Trasher Orphanage is the longest-running private ministry in Egypt.

But that's not all.

Lillian did her best to prepare children for their lives outside the institution. All orphanage residents shared responsibilities in the home, such as caring for the younger children, looking after animals on the small farm, doing laundry, and so on. A few were mentored in higher-level orphanage operations. This was the case for a young man named George and a young lady named Fathia. Lillian must have sensed that each had a unique calling in life. She placed George in charge of orphanage accounting and administration. Later, he was appointed to serve as orphanage pastor. Separately, Fathia ran special errands for Lillian, exposing her to Lillian's decision-making processes and responsibilities.

In addition to developing George's and Fathia's skills, Lillian carefully engineered opportunities for the two to interact with each other. This match-making effort worked: George and Fathia fell in love. Not long after, the two got married, and George was formally ordained as a Christian minister. The young couple moved to Beirut, Lebanon, where they served as missionaries for eleven years.

Then, at the height of Lebanon's civil war, George and Fathia and their young family fled their Beirut apartment. With the clothes on their backs and a few meager belongings, they secured a flight back to Egypt. The family returned to the orphanage in Assiout, where they were provided temporary lodging. A year passed, the war raged on, and George and Fathia wondered how long this strange in-between would last.

Soon thereafter, the orphanage board of directors asked George and Fathia to take the helm of the Lillian Trasher Orphanage. They agreed. Sixteen years after Lillian's death, George and Fathia began investing in the lives of children, just as Lillian had raised and invested in them. Over the course of the next four decades, they cared for ten thousand more children, widows, and blind women. Like Lillian Trasher, George and Fathia were portraits of faith and perseverance.

This incredible couple were not just the caretakers of, mentors to, and advocates for thousands of children. George and Fathia Assad are Joseph's parents, my in-laws. The legacy of Lillian Trasher's courageous steps out of the comfort zone and into the unknown set in motion an organization that has cared for the needs of more than twenty thousand people and touched thousands more. Lillian's, George's, and Fathia's strength in meeting every obstacle with integrity and dedication is what kept the home afloat all of those years and made an impact beyond words.

Lillian Trasher guided the orphanage through its first fifty years, and George and Fathia ushered the home through to its one-hundred-year anniversary in February 2011. After a lifetime of service, George went to heaven in May 2011, and Fathia joined him there in July 2013. They both diligently worked in the orphanage until an hour or two before their passings.

Remember when we talked about flipping the negative and making space for a transformation to occur?

Lillian's orphanage might not have been established and her purpose not realized had she not been given an ultimatum by the missionaries: "Either the baby goes, or you both go." This line-in-the-sand moment infused Lillian with the outrage she needed to do the outrageous thing she was meant to do. If George and Fathia had not dodged bullets to flee the war in Beirut, they wouldn't have found themselves back at the orphanage at a time when the home needed new leadership.

If Joseph hadn't been refused admission to a university in Egypt because of his Christian activities, he wouldn't have come to the United States for an education, become a US citizen, or served his new country as a CIA counterterrorism officer. If I had gotten any one of the hundreds of jobs I had applied for after college, I would not have applied to the CIA while studying at Georgetown. And if that hadn't happened, I would not have had the opportunity to help save lives and have the learning experiences that generated the ideas for this book.

When you transform your perceptions of what a successful path should be, you realize that hard things are the launchpads from which you are propelled to your place of purpose. Obstacles are the means by which you rise. Therefore, don't despise the small beginnings or underestimate the power of the simple steps you take to break inertia and move yourself forward. Every bold step counts. Every doubt you conquer, every fear you face, and every uncertainty you overcome by taking action gets you closer to where you need to be.

When you launch yourself off the X, you cause ripples that extend farther than you can see. Any action you take today has the power to change what happens not only tomorrow but far beyond tomorrow as well. When you change the focus or direction of your life, you will influence others, who will influence others …

Remember, we're not here to fit in or succumb to the status quo. We're not here to wither on the vine or color in the lines. We're not here to do things as everyone else does, because "that's the way it's always been done."

We're called to get off the X and change the world.

ACKNOWLEDGMENTS

After the publication of my first book, *Breaking Cover*, I was inundated by people telling me how much those stories inspired them to do hard things and get off the X, the title of chapter 8. Based on that feedback, I knew this concept really resonated. Readers and event audiences have repeated those words back to me—sometimes years after reading the book or after I've spoken from the stage about the importance of getting out of our personal and professional comfort zones.

Yet readers and event participants wanted more; they asked for tangible ways to overcome obstacles as they pursue their paths of purpose. They wanted to know how to operationalize their desire to get off the X. I have these readers to thank for triggering my desire to write another book that provides a methodology for getting unstuck and fulfilling your life's mission. This book is for you!

Strategies are helpful, but what makes them come alive are personal stories that demonstrate how people use those methodologies to move from struggle to success. That is why I decided to blend experiences from my spy and international consulting careers with those of people in my direct orbit. I wanted to provide readers with firsthand intelligence of what it looks like to take on a variety of obstacles in a variety of situations.

I would like to thank all the incredibly generous men and women who let me share their personal stories of how they got off the X. Their fortitude in the face of overwhelming difficulties motivates me every day. They triumphed over terrorism, religious persecution, teenage pregnancy, a toxic marriage, a severe learning disability, unexpected job loss, and profound amnesia. They persevered despite being kidnapped, used as a human shield by a dictator, and trapped as a hostage in a war zone.

My friends and family featured in this book would not take no for an answer. They were told they *couldn't* or *shouldn't*, but they *did*. They were told that their courses of action were unwise or their goals unattainable. But they took risks and defied the odds. Thank you to the following superstars who rebelled against their circumstances to get off the X and permitted me to use their stories to encourage others to do the same: Joseph Assad, Julie Clow, Nerina Campbell, Lucy Assad, Lisa Webb, John Adams, Glenn Coleman, Michelle Hougland, Paul and Kelsey Tompkins, and Bill Yeargin. I hope the way I have told your stories has honored you and your journeys.

Glenn Coleman became a friend after he sponsored an event for *Breaking Cover* in 2019 at the Cocoa Beach Public Library. I was not only blown away when I learned of his experience in Iraq, but I was also amazed by his optimism and humility. I was honored that he let me incorporate his story in this book. He was never able to get a memoir published, but he sent me a treasure trove of notes, writings, and other records he kept during his captivity in Iraq and reflections of that time after his return. This prepared me for a couple of phone interviews with him, where he related additional details of that experience. The last time I saw Glenn, in March 2024, he told me he was technically in hospice, but he was "still getting off the X." I had no doubt he was doing exactly that. Glenn passed away at the age of eighty-seven on May 13, 2024. I hope his life and memory inspire you as they have inspired me.

Lillian Trasher's story has always touched the deepest part of my soul. She remains a shining light of what it means to demonstrate love through service and sacrifice. Her legacy is vast, affecting tens of thousands of lives, including mine. While some people in the Christian community know about Lillian Trasher, few know the struggles she faced to follow her unorthodox calling. It's that part of the journey I find most compelling. Had she given up when circumstances got rough and obstacles abounded, the world would be a very different place.

I am also deeply indebted to my in-laws, George and Fathia Assad, who assumed the mantle of leadership and kept Lillian's legacy of faith going until their last hours on this earth. Thank you for modeling what dedication, deep faith, and resilience look like in action. Your service to God, your family, tens of thousands of Egyptians, and the wider international community inspires me every day. I hope Joseph and I have made you proud.

All my love and gratitude go to my husband, Joseph, without whom I would not have gotten off the X of my small town and traveled the world. Together we've learned the hard lessons of life and taken on a litany of obstacles in a bid to do whatever God has called us to. Nothing about this walk has been easy, but it has always been worth it. Thank you for modeling the controlled-detonation strategy you have used to such great effect throughout your life. I have learned so much by watching your gifts in motion, as you run and gun at those obstacles. I am indebted to you for the unwavering support to write this book and get it published. Without your encouragement, extremely productive brainstorming sessions, and editing assistance, this book would not exist. I pray that the strategy to get off the X, which we developed together in our very unconventional lives, will help others pursue the mission before them.

Thank you to the following crew who provided critical prayer support and encouragement for my latest mission—to produce and publish this book: my parents Art and Crystal Rigby, Julie Clow, Stephanie Prewitt, Jenna Balthazar, Mary Prediletto, Nerina Campbell, Michelle Hougland, Michelle Stewart, Brad and

Jennifer Graber, Chuck and Brandy Crisafulli, Kyle Newman and family, Jenny Blake, and Steve and Sue Clapp.

Jobi Jones, I heard the call from God to write the book, but knowing what a huge endeavor that would be, I asked God for a confirmation. Days later, you provided that confirmation at lunch by asking, completely out of the blue, "What's the title of your next book?" I almost fell out of my chair. Then God gave Joseph a dream the same night. Without his knowing anything about my prayer or your confirmation, he said, "Last night I dreamed you wrote another book." Thank you both for being sensitive to God and his leading. I don't think it could get any clearer than that.

Thank you to the extremely talented publishing crew at Dexterity Books. CEO and publisher extraordinaire Matt West embraced this mission because he is a master of getting off the X. I am grateful that Matt was willing to take on this book and help others conquer whatever is holding them back. Matt's deep knowledge of the publishing industry and his commitment to excellence and collaboration have benefited this book at every turn.

As all authors know well, a book is nothing without a crackerjack editor. Diane McDougall has been the answer to that prayer. Thank you, Diane, for toiling on this manuscript. You and Matt are gifted at working with authors to shape a book to make it the best it can be. I am blessed to have you on my team.

To all those secret agents out there who are ready to teach others what they have learned about getting off the X, it's time for an X revolution! My prayer is that this book sparks a fire that cannot be extinguished in all who read it, and who, in turn, pass on that unquenchable drive to all they encounter.

NOTES

1 "Actions on the Objective—Ambush," United States Army Infantry School, Fort Moore, accessed October 24, 2024, https://www.moore.army.mil/Infantry/DoctrineSupplement/ATP3-21.8/.

2 *Merriam-Webster*, s.v. "intimidate," accessed July 15, 2024, https://www.merriam-webster.com/dictionary/intimidate/.

3 Carly Vandergriendt, "The Dunning-Kruger Effect Explained," Healthline, updated March 11, 2022, https://www.healthline.com/health/dunning-kruger-effect/.

4 Ibid.

5 Ibid.

6 Rich Karlgaard, *Late Bloomers: The Power of Patience in a World Obsessed with Early Achievement* (New York: Broadway Books, 2019), 33.

7 Bill Yeargin, *Education of a CEO: Lessons for Leaders* (Fresno, CA: Ignite Press, 2021) 5–6.

8 Britta K. Hölzel et al., "Neural Mechanisms of Symptom Improvements in Generalized Anxiety Disorder Following Mindfulness Training," *NeuroImage: Clinical* 2 (2013): 448–58, https://doi.org/10.1016/j.nicl.2013.03.011.

9 Barry Schwartz, *The Paradox of Choice: Why More Is Less—How the Culture of Abundance Robs Us of Satisfaction* (New York: Ecco, 2016), 103.

10 Dan DeSena et al., "Behavioral Activation for Depression," University of Michigan Medicine Department of Psychiatry

Adult Patient Manual, accessed July 15, 2024, https://psych.med.umich.edu/anxiety-program/pdf/Behavioral-Activation-for-Depression.pdf.

11 Therapist Aid, "Behavioral Activation Treatment Guide," accessed July 15, 2024, https://www.therapistaid.com/therapy-guide/behavioral-activation-guide/.

12 Olivia Guy-Evans, "Brain Reward System," Simple Psychology, updated September 14, 2023, www.simplypsychology.org/brain-reward-system.html.

13 Chris Wallace, *Countdown Bin Laden: The Untold Story of the 247-Day Hunt to Bring the Mastermind of 9/11 to Justice* (New York: Avid Reader Press, 2021), 78–79.

14 Frans Johansson, *The Medici Effect: Breakthrough Insights at the Intersection of Ideas, Concepts, and Cultures* (Boston: Harvard Business School Press: 2004).

15 Gregory Berns, *Iconoclast: A Neuroscientist Reveals How to Think Differently* (Boston: Harvard Business Press, 2008) 33.

16 Janet and Geoff Benge, *Lillian Trasher: The Greatest Wonder in Egypt* (Seattle: YWAM Publishing, 2004), 44–45.

17 Ibid., 65.

18 Ibid., 189.

19 Martha Beck, "Find Your Purpose and Power: Rediscovering Your Superhero Self," *Martha's Blog*, December 11, 2018, https://marthabeck.com/2014/06/find-your-purpose-and-power/.

20 Sylvie Droit-Volet and Warren H. Meck, "How Emotions Colour Our Perception of Time," *Trends in Cognitive Sciences* 11, no. 12 (December 2007): 504–13, https://doi.org/10.1016/j.tics.2007.09.008.

21 Amandine E. Rey et al., "Pain Dilates Time Perception," *Scientific Reports* 7, no. 1 (2017), https://doi.org/10.1038/s41598-017-15982-6.

22 Susan E. Coldwell et al., "Temporal Information Reduces Children's Pain Reports during a Multiple-Trial Cold Pressor Procedure," *Behavior Therapy* 33, no. 1 (2002): 45–63, https://doi.org/10.1016/s0005-7894(02)80005-3.

23 Jenny Blake, *Pivot: The Only Move That Matters Is Your Next One* (New York: Portfolio/Penguin, 2016), 135.

24 Charlotte Nickerson, "Emotional Contagion: What It Is and How to Avoid It," Simple Psychology, updated November 8, 2021, www.simplypsychology.org/what-is-emotional-contagion.html.

25 Andrew L. Thomson and Jason T. Siegel, "Elevation: A Review of Scholarship on a Moral and Other-Praising Emotion," *Journal of Positive Psychology* 12, no. 6 (2016): 628–38, https://doi.org/10.1080/17439760.2016.1269184.

26 Simone Schnall, Jean Roper, and Daniel M.T. Fessler, "Elevation Leads to Altruistic Behavior," *Psychological Science* 21, no. 3 (2010): 315–20, https://doi.org/10.1177/0956797609359882.

ABOUT THE AUTHOR

Hailing from a small town and simple beginnings, Michele has repeatedly conquered her tendency to freeze by pushing herself to get off the beaten path and do hard things. Her proficiency in getting off the X resulted in her recruitment by the CIA months before the September 11 attacks. After graduating from Georgetown University, she became an undercover CIA intelligence officer and spent ten years specializing in counterterrorism and counterintelligence in war zones and other dangerous locations.

Michele's five tours in the Arab world and travel to more than fifty countries have given her the experience needed to serve as a successful corporate adviser, security specialist, and author with an unparalleled understanding of how to operate in tough places. This extensive overseas expertise informs her ability to deal with the most challenging people, including terrorists and insurgents—experiences which are highlighted in her bestselling memoir *Breaking Cover: My Secret Life in the CIA and What It Taught Me about What's Worth Fighting For* (Tyndale Momentum, 2018).

Michele and her husband, Joseph, left the CIA after a decade to run a boutique advisory firm providing operational advice, negotiation and mediation assistance, risk assessments, vetting, and investigation support for companies working in the Middle East, Europe, and the United States.

Because she understands the difficulty of punching through fear, doubt, intimidation, and insecurity, Michele is passionate about showing others how they can get off the X and live out their dreams. She has provided training and delivered keynotes for a wide variety of clients, including Morgan Stanley, Google, Disney, and the Smithsonian.

Michele holds a master's degree in contemporary Arab studies from Georgetown University School of Foreign Service and an undergraduate political science degree from Palm Beach Atlantic University. She lives in Central Florida.